ACCLAIM FOR
NOT JUST QUOTES
INSPIRATION FOR THE EVER-EVOLVING WOMAN
BY DOROTHY SANDER

"Dorothy writes from her heart, and she articulates what many women think and feel but struggle to put into words. This book is a combination of her hard-earned wisdom and quotations that succinctly capture the essence of what it is to be human. Whether you sit down and read it cover to cover or select a particular section that has meaning for you, it's a must-read as well as a perfect gift for any woman in your life."

— **Candace Johnson,** *Editor & Writer*

"If you're like me, you have books that you go back to again and again for solace, assurance, new ideas, confirmation, or to break through mental blocks. *Not Just Quotes: Inspiration for the Ever-evolving Woman* is one such book. Dorothy Sander shares not only personal insights, but quotes that support them from some of the world's greatest teachers. This book is an invaluable resource."

—Lucinda Sage-Midgorden, *Writer, Teacher, Author*

"Dorothy Sander shares inspiration and wisdom in this book of quotes. With each topic, she writes something from her own experience and knowledge and then has several people's quotes to reinforce the ideas. It's one of those books that you can just pick up, open to a page and get some goodies, or, you can sit down and read the whole thing cover to cover."

—Laurie Schur, *Psychotherapist, Director & Producer of the "Beauty of Aging Film Project"*

11066 68995

"A beautifully written book which stays with us long after it's been read. Sander inspires us with her wisdoms about aging with grace - the hardships and the beauty. She delves into what many women begin to question about things and feelings that change as we age and how we become from our experiences. Each chapter is followed by some inspirational quotes that we can go back to whenever we may feel the need for some uplifting."

—**D.G. Kaye**, *Author of Conflicted Hearts*

"Not Just Quotes by Dorothy Sander encourages the reader to ponder who they are and who they can become. For women and men both, it is a book that can be read from beginning to end or by just looking at any given page and selecting a quote to ponder. Written clearly and with sensitivity, this book allows people of all faiths -- or frankly none -- to reflect upon the purpose(s) of why we are here, where we may be headed and how best to get to where we want to go."

—**Dr. Eric Mondschein**, *Educational Consultant & Author of "Life at 12 College Road"*

I highly recommend *Not Just Quotes, Inspiration for the Ever-Evolving Woman* by Dorothy Sander. In this well-written book, she reflects on life challenges, following each with motivational quotes from many. For this to be my midlife journey, I would have to live to 154, yet I find the writings still relate to my continuing journey. The book is a gem to keep close for re-reading. It is like a balm to soothe the rough edges of life."

—**E.E. Wilder**, *Author of The Spruce Gum Tree*

ALSO BY THE AUTHOR

Pathways to Wisdom (Coming Soon!)
From Upheaval & Change to a More Peaceful You

Caring for Mom
Midlife Reflections (2010)

*"I admire the author's wisdom, insight, perspective, and
ability to put into words what so many of us feel
and are unable to articulate."*
—Maria Maggi, *Editor*

NOT JUST QUOTES

*Inspiration for the
Ever-Evolving Woman*

DOROTHY SANDER

Published by
Aging Abundantly Press

ISBN-13: 978-1986734370
ISBN-10: 1986734374

For information about bulk purchase discounts, please contact Aging Abundantly Special Sales, AgingAbundantly@gmail.com

Cover Design by Jill Davis

Aging Abundantly Press
Durham, NC 27712
www.AgingAbundantly.com

DEDICATION

Not Just Quotes is dedicated to all the women throughout history who have had the courage to show up, speak up, and stand up for what matters most.

To the women of the Aging Abundantly Community who enrich my life and broaden my perspective a little more each passing day: you give me hope, and it is an honor to walk beside you into the wilderness of life after fifty. As you listen, share, encourage and love one another, you carry on the legacy of women who have, throughout time, created a safe and accepting place for all who enter there.

I also dedicate this book to the women who have participated in the many conversations over the last decade about what it means to be a woman over fifty today. You have collectively helped expand our cultures awareness and broadened its perspective. Even though there is still work to be done, we are in a much better place. Thank you, Suzanne, Sue Ann, Christy, Celia, Jill, Laurie, Frankie, Crystal, Marsha, Bonnie, Libby, Bonnie, Mary, Lisa, Sylvia, Carolyn, Diane, Sue, Lisa, Joan, Robin, Sophie, Elizabeth, Kay, Vicki, Ceri, Sandy, Chris, Ann, Heather, Holly, Rita, Madeline, Dale, Barbara, Hope, Nancy, Marian, CJ, Julia, Maggie, Dana, Joan, Sparrow, and so many others.

To two fierce and brilliant women whose words and teachings guided me, and countless others, on the path of spiritual healing; from Jungian theory to a conscious life, Caroline Myss and Dr. Clarissa Pinkola Estés, you have changed me from the inside out. In addition, you are invaluable role models of courage without end, love without qualifications, and strength and perseverance that shine a spot light on the true beauty of the feminine nature.

DJS

"*Just when the caterpillar thought her world was over, she became a butterfly.*"

~ Barbara Haines Howett, author,
Ladies of the Borobudur

PREFACE

"Speak, even when no one is listening."

I am fascinated by questions and ideas that live just beyond our conscious mind's ability to answer them. These questions push us in directions we cannot perceive in advance. They stretch us and grow us beyond the rational mind's ability to direct.

Looking outside the obvious is my calling, despite my best efforts to walk a different path. Each time I turn my back on the quest for enlightenment, circumstances return me to swiftly, and sometimes abruptly, to the uneasy road of self-discovery and the search for answers to universal questions.

If we are to address life's biggest questions, we cannot do so by skimming the surface of life. We must dig deep and use all the tools that at our disposal. Each of us was born with all that we need to move toward greater awareness, whatever that might look like for each of us as individuals. We simply must choose to do so.

We are each of us born with imagination, intuition, faith, and more than anything else, courage. Sometimes we believe that life has beaten it out of us, but this cannot be so, for our core soul self cannot be altered. Shoved far beneath the surface and layered with masks, it still lies quietly in waiting for us to discover.

When I say this, I do not say without the awareness that it is not an easy road, nor a direct one. But, in my humble opinion, it is a path worth the agony it can reveal.

When I talk about wrestling with life's questions, I am not talking about a casual, intellectual reflection on philosophical and theological questions over a drink with a friend. I am talking about living the questions, living them in such a way that they draw what lies outside of our awareness in the light of day. It means waking up to our shadow selves and daring to venture into the darkness where these aspects of ourselves live. It is a profound opportunity to find the healing path that will mend our broken places and unify us, body, mind and spirit.

SYMBOLIC LANGUAGE

Symbolic language is a powerful tool and useful in such an inquiry. Symbols carry within them truths that are both universal and specific. That point us to a thing that is often outside of our immediate awareness or bigger than our ability to quantity. It's like looking into to outer space at night. We see a few specific stars, but there are still an infinite number that we can only barely see, or not see at all.

Symbolism is the language of the unconscious and when we explore symbols we step into a place that is at the edge of our present understanding. Dwelling in symbolic language invites us to take the next step in our personal evolution.

It is no surprise to me that quotes are so popular today. We live in a time when we are desperate to make sense of the chaotic world we live in. We long for universal truths that we can grab hold of and find an anchor. The symbols, once delivered by our religious, governmental, business and family institutions, are no longer relevant to us. Yet, we yearn, and always will, for meaning, purpose and a sense of belonging. We need symbolic language and guidance to lead us where our soul knows it needs to go.

As a writer I spend my days searching for just the right word to express a thought or a feeling or convey the depth of an experience. It is a frustrating endeavor at times! Many words are subject to interpretation and nuance. The word intended may be misunderstood or heard in a way the author doesn't intend.

When I look for a quote to convey a thought, even I am one step removed from the author's intent. Then, I hand it off to the reader, who may take something different still from the words. Certain quotes, however, resonate universally. I believe it is this universal nature of some quotes that make them so popular and powerful. They speak to the heart of life's questions to all. Even if what we take away is slightly different person to person, the universal nature of the quote inspires all to ask the questions.

A LITTLE HISTORY

I began gathering quotes in earnest when I reinvented myself as a writer at fifty. As a product of the 60's, I was among the many women who were in the initial stages of the struggle to come to terms with what it meant to be viable women as we aged. We were entering our parent's world as "senior citizens", but we did not want to be like them!

I started writing a blog called "Aging Abundantly" that eventually became what is now the foundation for The Aging Abundantly Community. When I added the Aging Abundantly Facebook page, I began to post quotes because they provided a quick easy way to impart important values and beliefs I was in the midst of revisiting. They carried weight and import in a simple format.

I only posted quotes that were meaningful to me. I was not surprised when others were drawn to them as well. Now, however, I believe there is a deeper reason for their popularity: we are a people starved for a deeper connection to ourselves, to each other and to the universe. Quotes that called to me then were speaking to the deepest part of me, to my soul, if you will. And what calls to the soul is universal ~ in that regard, we all speak the same language.

I put together my first quote book, the *Little Book of Quotes*, later revised and expanded for Kindle® as

Finding Hope, to give readers something tangible that they could keep with them and refer to often. Quotes should be read more than once. When we live with and reflect on a quote over time, we open ourselves to its deepest and broadest meaning for us. As a result, we change, we grow, we become more aware of what has meaning and value to us.

This version of the quote book is designed for the woman facing the challenging issues and questions that often arise when we enter our middle years. They may be questions we thought we had sufficiently addressed in our teens and early twenties, but twenty years of living has reshaped our answers.

In the fifth decade, all hell breaks loose with the onset of menopause, children leaving home and the empty nest appears. We are entering a process of metamorphosis that will usher in a new life. That is why I chose the butterfly quote way back when to use in the header of my blog. We are very much like cocooning soon-to-be butterflies at this stage in our life. Just as the moth melts down within the cocoon, we too have the opportunity to dive into the transformation process when our external life seems to be disintegrating.

I have also included some of my own thoughts, many written during this period of my life.

HOW TO READ A QUOTE

A quote we love is usually one that speaks to something deep inside of us. We grasp it first with our intuition, and then, if we open the door to it, it moves to our heart and speaks to our soul. It is asking us to consider it, to ask, "how does this apply to me and to the choices I have before me?".

You might read a quote and say, "Oh, that's nice! That resonates, makes me feel good, stirs something in me." But then it's forgotten. You must ask the next question, and the next. You might ask yourself questions such as:

- What about this quote capture my attention?
- What is it telling me? What do I think about what it's saying?
- What might I take from this quote into my day-to-day life?
- How is it inspiring me to change?
- What soul truth(s) is it drawing my attention to?

To get the most out of a quote, follow where it leads. A quote speaks to us because it touches something beyond our immediate awareness. That "something" is asking to be brought out into the open so that we might change, grow and be transformed into the person we were born to be. As we think about the quote's meaning, we will gradually become aware of its deeper more personal meaning. The process reshapes us and our evolution continues.

CONTENTS

INTRODUCTION

Since the beginning of recorded history, human beings have struggled to make sense of life. We long to understand why things happen as they do and if there is meaning and purpose in in our suffering.

A deep sense that we have something unique to offer the world strains toward expression. Inherent in this is a fundamental yearning for love and connection. We long to cross the divide between solitude and intimacy.

These natural human longings rise to the surface during times of transition, change and challenge. As the past stretches out behind us, and the future shrinks, age-old questions become more urgent. We long to live a congruent life, to give voice to the music within us before our time on earth is up.

Change and upheaval creates the perfect opportunity for positive change. Each challenge we face gives us the exact ingredients we need to resolve our inner incongruencies and conflicts, and the opportunity to choose a more authentic path.

It makes sense to turn to teachers, writers, and students of human nature and spirituality who have traveled this road before us. It is interesting to note that collectively their messages are ones that sing in unison, and support of universal truths and principles.

I hope that you will discover more about yourself and your relationship to truth as you peruse these pages. May you gain clarity, vision and the wisdom necessary to nurture your ability and willingness to sing your own beautiful song ~ the world needs you.

CHANGE

Change is a natural part of life. Yet many of us find the uncertainty of it uncomfortable. It is challenging and often frightening. This may be especially true as so many of us have experienced great hurts and disappointments in our lives to date. Wounded, we gravitate toward the status quo.

The problem with giving in to our rigidity is that we deny the natural forward motion of our creative life force and something in us dies. Our reality grows dark and the future terrifying.

Mistakes and misfortunates are valuable teachers, when we do not allow them the power to control us.

Midlife is about change and much of this change is about endings. Our jobs as full time Mom, daughter, goddess to our spouse (or whatever role our youthful self has played in our romantic relationship), and career woman has suddenly morphed into something quite different. Looming large for many women is loss of our youthful body and all it possessed.

With all these endings taking place outside of our control, we must allow ourselves the time and space to grieve. Staying open to the grieving process is essential to the metamorphosis process. If we shove away this uncomfortable feelings and plow forward in some new direction, we do ourselves a disservice. When we stay open and aware of the process we are going through, we release its energy from our bodies, minds and spirit and creating space for what is to come.

It is a process that is at once heart wrenching and liberating. Many conflicting emotions keep us off balance, but allowing the conflict enables us to change and move on.

When we find our house is empty of children, we long to embrace the "extra" time, but instead we find that it overwhelms us. We don't know what to do! We feel lost and without purpose or direction. The external demands that once shaped our days have vanished, and we are adrift in a sea of possibilities.

As we begin to struggle with our changing bodies another aspect of our identity is suddenly on shifting ground. What now of my "womanhood"? My femininity? My ability to use my gender as leverage? What does it mean to be a woman when our body ages? Who will we be when our external appearance is transformed by time? How will this change affect our relationships with the men in our lives, or the women?

For many, careers that once held our attention, are no longer as compelling. For those who set aside career aspirations to raise children, a new eagerness to refocus on this path may arise, but we are so much older! We've been out of the workforce for so long, how will we fit in? Can we fit in? Is it too late?

Women who have careers with several decades invested, often find they are being replaced by younger people. Or, what they worked so hard to attain, no longer seems meaningful or worthwhile. For some, a sense that things didn't turn out the way they dreamed, disappointment can quickly morph into depression.

Questions arise. What now? If I give up the dream I held for so long, what will I do? Where will I find my meaning and purpose? What will inspire me to get up in the morning? Should I start over? Head in a different direction? Retire? If I retire, then what?

All this change is felt in our relationships as well. The dynamics in marriages change. Children become the central focus in many relationships. After twenty plus years of a child-focused marriage, an empty nest leaves many couples reeling.

When we decide to care for aging parents, the demands on the relationship also increase.

Menopause interferes with our once easy sex life, creating another obstacle to the path of closeness in our relationship with our significant other.

All these changes ignite an endless stream of questions.

- Is my marriage still viable?
- How has our relationship changed? What steps can we take to try to reconnect?
- Should I care for my aging parents?
- How much of myself should I give to the process?
- How do I handle being responsible for the person(s) who was once responsible for me?
- Who am I, now that my parents are gone?
- How do I show up for my children and still allow them the freedom to make their own decisions and mistakes?
- What is my place in their lives now, and what is my responsibility for maintaining it?
- Do my children still need me? Do they even want me in their lives?
- What do I want my relationship with my children, their spouses and children to be?
- Do I want to get involved with the care of my grandchildren? In what capacity?

Although the focus and particulars of the lives we once lived may be dissolving, we have unaware been forging pearls of a different sort. It's time to pull them out and see what we have learned. We should and must take this splendid opportunity of discomfort and uncertainty to reflect on all that we have learned and bring into awareness our desires for the next portion of our life. The metamorphosis has begun.

Deep diving into ourselves demands that we

remain open and courageous to whatever arises. This is not easy for we have spent a lifetime building walls of protection to minimize our suffering and keep going. We resist removing them and yet it is time. These walls and masks have served their purpose. Now we must let them go and find our true selves once again.

As we dig through the chunks of coal and ash, we will find the jewels that have been formed in the oven of our steps and missteps. This is the process of transformation. metamorphosis. If we are open and have courage, we can navigate these significant transitions in a way that changes us and challenges us to grow in our authenticity. The greater the difficulty, the richer the transformation process.

The challenges we face are exactly the ones we need to grow. In fact, they are a personally designed recipe for significant growth and lasting change. We are given exactly what we need -- no more and no less.

We are called to let go of the drive, ambition and expectation of our youth, and shift our focus from the external world to the internal one. There we will discover the many gifts of the aging process -- gifts that will guide and sustain us through the remainder of our lives.

Finding our way through the maze of disintegration and reformation required for significant personal growth is an important task at midlife. It is also important to remember that it is a process that takes time and attention. We do not have to choose this path, but if we do not choose it, it will continue to reappear in various forms, whether we like it or not, and it will do so with ever increasing urgency until the day we die.

Just as the caterpillar must struggle to break free from her chrysalis, so we, too, must struggle to break free from our perceptions of how life is supposed to be, and learn to live it as it is.

There are many authors, teachers, and experts who have traveled this road before us. Take advantage of their wisdom.

REFLECT on CHANGE

*What has changed in your life? How has it changed your life? How has this change affected how you see yourself?*_____

_____

_____

_____

_____

_____

_____

*What steps are you taking to adapt to this change?*_____

_____

_____

_____

_____

*What do you miss most?*_____

_____

_____

*What would you like to create in the empty space?*_____

_____

_____

_____

_____

_____

QUOTES ON CHANGE

"When the voice and the vision on the inside is more profound, and more clear and loud than all opinions on the outside, you've begun to master your life."

~John Demartini, American author,
Count Your Blessings: The Healing Power of
Gratitude and Love

"If we go slowly and steadily, go where our hearts desire, find ways to get back to places we love, do the things we love to do—slow and steadily, magic happens."

~Martha Beck, American sociologist & author

"A vision is not just a picture of what could be; it is an appeal to our better selves, a call to become something more."

~Rosabeth Moss Kanter, American professor,
Harvard Business School

"I never panic when I get lost. I just change where it is I want to go."

~Rita Rudner, American comedian & writer

"All my life I used to wonder what I would become when I grew up. Then, about seven years ago, I realized that I was never going to grow up—that growing is an ever-ongoing process."

~M. Scott Peck, American psychiatrist & author,
The Road Less Traveled

"Just let go. Let go of how you thought your life should be, and embrace the life that is trying to work its way into your consciousness."

~Caroline Myss, American teacher & author, Medical Intuitive

"Very often a change of self is needed more than a change of scene."

~Arthur Christopher Benson, British author

"Look at everything as though you were seeing it either for the first or last time. Then your time on earth will be filled with glory."

~Betty Smith, American author, A Tree Grows in Brooklyn

"Truth is tough. It will not break, like a bubble, at a touch, nay, you may kick it all about all day like a football, and it will be round and full at evening."

~Oliver Wendell Holmes, Jr., Associate Supreme Court Justice

"If we could change ourselves, the tendencies in the world would also change. As man changes his own nature, so does the attitude of the world change towards him."

~Mahatma Gandhi, leader of India's Independence Movement

"Clinging to the past is the problem. Embracing change is the solution."

~Gloria Steinem, American journalist & author

"The process of metamorphosis is scary and sometimes painful but is also the way to experience wonderful new adventures we weren't even able to imagine in our caterpillar identities. Accept the process: care for yourself, dream big, work hard, and keep learning. Then don't be surprised when one morning, you wake up to find that you have wings."

~Martha Beck, American sociologist & author

"There can be only one permanent revolution – a moral one -- the regeneration of the inner man. How is this revolution to take place? Nobody knows how it will take place in humanity, but every man feels it clearly in himself. And yet in our world everybody thinks of changing humanity, and nobody thinks of changing himself."

~Leo Tolstoy, Russian author,
"Three Methods of Reform" in Pamphlets
(translated from the Russian)

"Change will not come if we wait for some other person or some other time. We are the ones we've been waiting for. We are the change that we seek."

~Barack Obama, 44th President of the United States

BEAUTY

"What does it mean to be a woman when the beauty of my youth is fading?" we ask.

"How can I consider myself feminine and attractive when my skin is sagging, and wrinkles crease my eyes?"

"Does my partner still find me desirable? How can I believe that he does? Do I still care?"

We struggle with what it means to be beautiful as we age. As young women, our external appearance seemed paramount in importance. We believed that how we looked determined our fortune (or misfortune) in both love and life. We worked on our "look," whether it was professional, sexy, or sophisticated. We did this at least as much, if not more than work on who we were on the inside. Our looks were both our defense and offense as we faced daily challenges.

At some point, we began to sense that the game was changing. The power and influence of our appearance and our ability to shape it was changing. The parameters were different. The edge of youth was no longer ours to manage. At first, we barely noticed.

Now, we can't *not* notice.

Is it time to relinquish this enormous piece of ourselves? Who will we be without it? Will we suddenly disappear into thin air and no longer matter? As old women will we become invisible and powerless?

Or is it time to look at beauty in a unique way? Perhaps the belief that women over fifty are no longer sexy or beautiful is simply a cultural belief and not fact at all.

What exactly is beauty? Is there not more to it than perfect skin and a perfect body? Is it not more than the makeup we apply and the clothes we wear? What is it that truly shapes beauty?

Does beauty not shine forth from a wrinkled face as surely as it does from a smooth one? Does the twinkle in the eye of a wise and serene old woman not grab our hearts? Doesn't it pull us in more profoundly than a young, inexperienced woman walking into a room?

Life lived, scars born, the sincerity and serenity of a smile playing on the lips of a woman who has really lived – Hers is a force to be reckoned with! Is a heart and soul who has survived decades of life and filled to overflowing with wisdom and love not beauty at its ripest and must abundant?

I think it is.

REFLECT on BEAUTY

What thoughts, feelings or judgements arise when you ask yourself, "Am I beautiful?"

_____

_____

_____

_____

_____

_____

_____

_____

_____

Do you remember the first time you thought each thought, or felt the feeling? What was going on?

_____

_____

_____

_____

_____

_____

_____

_____

_____

_____

_____

_____

_____

_____

_____

_____

QUOTES ON BEAUTY

"Beauty is not in the face; beauty is a light in the heart."

> *~Kahlil Gibran, Lebanese-American writer & poet,*
> *author of The Prophet*

"Although beauty may be in the eye of the beholder, the feeling of being beautiful exists solely in the mind of the beheld."

> *~Martha Beck, American sociologist & author*

"People don't remember the mistakes you have made or dark images you hold about yourself. They remember your beauty when you feel ugly; your wholeness when you are broken; your innocence when you feel guilty; and your purpose when you are confused."

> *~Alan Cohen, American author*

"As we grow old, the beauty steals inward."

> *~Ralph Waldo Emerson,*
> *American philosopher & essayist*

". . . flowers . . . are a proud assertion that a ray of beauty out values all the utilities of the world."

> *~Ralph Waldo Emerson,*
> *American philosopher & essayist, from "Gifts"*

"There is no cosmetic for beauty like happiness."

> *~ Maria Mitchell, American astronomer*

"Beauty is in the eye of the beholder, and it may be necessary from time to time to give a stupid or misinformed beholder a black eye."

~*Miss Piggy, philosopher,*
The Muppet Show

"Think of all the beauty still left around you and be happy."

~*Anne Frank, German diarist,*
The Diary of a Young Girl

A thing of beauty is a joy for ever:
Its loveliness increases; it will never
Pass into nothingness . . .

~*John Keats, English poet,*
"Endymion: Book I"

"A woman whose smile is open and whose expression is glad has a kind of beauty no matter what she wears."

~*Annie Roiphe, American writer & journalist*

"People are like stained-glass windows. They sparkle and shine when the sun is out, but when the darkness sets in, their true beauty is revealed only if there is a light from within."

~*Dr. Elisabeth Kubler-Ross, Swiss-American*
psychiatrist & author of On Death and Dying

"Beauty is whatever gives joy."

~*Edna St. Vincent Millay, American poet*

"The more we learn to communicate with our bodies, the more we may feel as though we're aging backward, like Merlin the Magician, becoming healthier and more comfortable in our skin with the passage of time."

~Martha Beck, American sociologist & author,
"The Body Whisperer"

"No matter how plain a woman may be, if truth and honesty are written across her face, she will be beautiful."

~Eleanor Roosevelt, former First Lady & author

"Let the beauty we love be what we do."

~Rumi, Persian poet & scholar,
"Spring Giddiness"

"To love beauty is to see light."

~Victor Hugo, French poet & author

"Beauty is eternity gazing at itself in a mirror."

~Khalil Gibran, Lebanese-American writer & poet,
The Prophet

"So much has been said and sung of beautiful girls. Why doesn't someone wake up to the beauty of old women?"

~Harriet Beecher Stowe,
American abolitionist & author

"The beauty of a woman must be seen from in her eyes, because that is the doorway to her heart, the place where love resides."

~ Audrey Hepburn, British actress & film star

"It is time for parents to teach young people early on that in diversity there is beauty and there is strength."

~ Maya Angelou, American poet & author

"Since love grows within you, so beauty grows. For love is the beauty of the soul."

~ Saint Augustine of Hippo,
Christian theologian & philosopher

"Let us live for the beauty of our own reality."

~ Charles Lamb, English writer & essayist

"Love built on beauty, soon as beauty, dies."

~ John Donne, English poet,
"Elegies: II. The Anagram"

FEAR

When we live in fear, we are not only robbed of the joy we can no longer see, but the texture and richness of our lives disappears. Fear calls to each one of us, but we do not have to answer. Though we may want to huddle in a corner of our lives when we feel the nudge of fear, we can choose instead to focus our attention on building courage and confidence.

It is true that a day doesn't go by that we don't hear of, or live through, some natural or unnatural disaster. We are privy to a stream of unrelenting destruction at the hands of our fellow human beings, and sometimes at our own hands. In a world overrun with messages of fear, how can we feel secure? How can we find the courage, day after day, to turn our faces toward hope and away from despair?

The surest way to break through the barrier of fear is to acknowledge and accept that the answer to fear is within us. We must look inside of ourselves to find our courage and the strength to face our fears. It will never be found in another person, a job, a political system or any other an external source. Courage is an inside job.

The good news is that we have everything we need right inside of us. We are powerful beyond our own imaginings and the spiritual forces that live within us will teach us what the world never can.

A force far greater than our fear exists, but it is up to us to tune in to it, to turn toward it again and again, and to acknowledge it. Our trust in it can only build over time. We learn to depend on its guidance as well as and the strength and courage it calls forth from us.

This internal power is something that we cannot touch with our hands and struggle to describe, but we know that it is there. We must lean into hope, as we lean away from fear.

External difficulties will threaten to defeat us, but our spirit lives on. Our bodies may fade, but all that is good and right and true will continue. It is alive wherever love exists.

Soak in the truth of the words of wisdom spoken in the pages of this book and be fortified. You are stronger than you know. You have more courage than you ever dreamed possible. Trust it. Dare to experience it. Allow yourself to grow into it, bit by bit.

RFLECT on FEAR

Think of a time when you felt fear. Tune into your body. What do you notice? Where do you feel fear? Is there a knot in your stomach, a tightness in your throat, a band around your head? Just notice.

_____
_____
_____
_____
_____
_____
_____
_____
_____
_____
_____

What thoughts arose with the fear? When was the first time you had that thought?

_____
_____
_____
_____
_____
_____
_____
_____
_____
_____
_____
_____
_____
_____

QUOTES ON FEAR

"Our deepest fear is not that we are inadequate. Our deepest fear is that we are powerful beyond measure. It is our light, not our darkness that most frightens us. We ask ourselves, "Who am I to be brilliant, gorgeous, talented, fabulous?" Actually, who are you not to be? You are a child of God. Your playing small does not serve the world. There is nothing enlightened about shrinking so that other people won't feel insecure around you. We are all meant to shine, as children do. We were born to make manifest the glory of God that is within us. It's not just in some of us; it's in everyone. And as we let our own light shine, we unconsciously give other people permission to do the same. As we are liberated from our own fear, our presence automatically liberates others."

~Marianne Williamson, American author,
A Return to Love: Reflections on the Principles
of a Course in Miracles

"Remember that it's okay to ask for help when you're stumped, because sometimes you really can't be expected to handle everything alone."

~Martha Beck, American sociologist & author

"You gain strength, courage, and confidence by every experience in which you really stop to look fear in the face. You must do the thing which you think you cannot do."

~Eleanor Roosevelt, former First Lady & author

"The enemy is fear. We think it is hate, but it is fear."
~Mahatma Gandhi, leader of
India's Independence Movement

"Getting over your fear without doing anything scary is like learning to swim before you go near the water—it would be nice if such a thing were possible, but it ain't."
~Martha Beck, American sociologist & author

"Fears are educated into us, and can, if we wish, be educated out."
~Karl Augustus Menninger, American psychiatrist

"Put your desires above your fears. Stop running and face it, whatever it is."
~Martha Beck, American sociologist & author,
Finding Your Own North Star: Living the Life

"Most of us live two lives. The life we live, and the unlived life within us. Between the two stands Resistance."
~Steven Pressfield, American author

"When you say or do anything to please, get, keep, influence, or control anyone or anything, fear is the cause and pain is the result."
~Byron Katie, American speaker & author,
Question Your Thinking, Change the World

"There are some things one can only achieve by a deliberate leap in the opposite direction. One has to go abroad in order to find the home one has lost."

~Franz Kafka, German-Bohemian writer

"No, I don't think that every fear is rational and all fears are good. I feel fear is neutral—it's how we channel it that makes it good or bad."

~Scott H. Young, American writer,
"Fear Is Good"

"Real life isn't always going to be perfect or go our way, but the recurring acknowledgement of what is working in our lives can help us not only to survive but surmount our difficulties."

~Sarah Ban Breathnach, American author of Simple Abundance, A Daybook of Comfort and Joy

"We must build dikes of courage to hold back the flood of fear."

~ Dr. Martin Luther King, Jr., American Baptist Minister & Civil Rights Movement activist, from his sermon "Antidotes for Fear"

"For where no hope is left, is left no fear."

~John Milton, English writer,
Paradise Lost

"Fear defeats more people than any other one thing in the world."

~Ralph Waldo Emerson,
American philosopher & essayist

"She stood in the storm, and when the wind did not blow her away, she adjusted her sails."
~Elizabeth Edwards, American attorney & author

"Don't be afraid of your fears. They're not there to scare you. They're there to let you know that something is worth it."
~ C. JoyBell C., American author

Fear is only as deep as the mind allows.
~Unknown

"Fear is the main source of superstition, and one of the main sources of cruelty. To conquer fear is the beginning of wisdom."
~ Bertrand Russell, British philosopher, Unpopular Essays

"You can discover what your enemy fears most by observing the means he uses to frighten you."
~ Eric Hoffer, American philosopher

"Who sees all beings in his own self, and his own self in all beings, loses all fear."
~ from the Hindu scripture, Isa Upanishad

You are only afraid if you are not in harmony with yourself. People are afraid because they have never owned up to themselves."
~ Hermann Hesse, German-born Swiss poet, novelist, & painter, author of Siddhartha

"Fear keeps us focused on the past or worried about the future. If we can acknowledge our fear, we can realize that right now we are okay. Right now, today, we are still alive, and our bodies are working marvelously. Our eyes can still see the beautiful sky. Our ears can still hear the voices of our loved ones."

~ *Thich Nhat Hanh, Vietnamese Buddhist Monk*

COURAGE

We can live our dreams. They are within our reach. No matter what our age or circumstances, we can find joy in our todays. We may have to give our dreams some breathing room. We may have to allow them to change shape a bit to fit our circumstances, but we do not have to abandon them.

What we must do is give up fear and despair. There are always 101 reasons why we really don't want to do the thing we think about doing. I'm the queen of negative thinking: ask my husband!

I wanted to write since the first time I held a pencil in my hand. I didn't begin to take that dream seriously until I was 50. Since that time, my dream has changed with circumstances, but I am now doing what I love to do. It's not perfect. Nothing is, but the value of pursuing your dreams comes from living from our heart, from the place where all dreams reside.

We all lack confidence to some degree or another. The bigger our hope, the harder it may be to risk. Many of us experienced childhoods that weakened us rather than giving us the necessary courage and freedom to learn, expand, and grab hold of opportunities. Our subsequent life experiences may have caused us to shrink further still. What I know to be true is this: it is never too late to follow your heart.

We can choose courage. We can choose to walk away from despair, hopelessness, defeat. We can reach deep inside and grab the tiniest corner of a dream waiting beneath the wreckage. We can hold on for dear life to that little bit of hope. And bit by bit, the dream finds its way to the surface of our life.

By making the decision to try again, to take the leap of faith one more time, we will make the decision to live in hope. There are no mistakes in life. There are only experiences from which we learn and move on. Every accomplishment begins with the decision to try.

REFLECT on COURAGE

List a time when you were courageous. How did you feel? Were you ever scared? What motivated you to act anyway?

_____

_____

_____

_____

_____

_____

_____

_____

_____

_____

How do you after? How did your choice to be courageous influence the situation or outcome?

_____

_____

_____

_____

_____

_____

_____

_____

_____

_____

_____

_____

QUOTES ON COURAGE

"Life's ups and downs provide windows of opportunity to determine your values and goals. Think of using all obstacles as stepping stones to build the life you want."

~Marsha Sinetar, American author,
To Build the Life You Want,
Create the Work You Love

"Go confidently in the direction of your dreams.
Live the life you've imagined."

~Henry David Thoreau, American essayist & writer,
Walden, or Life In the Woods

"There came a time when the risk to remain tight in the bud was more painful than the risk it took to blossom."

~Elizabeth Appell, American writer,
from a 1979 class theme, John F. Kennedy University
(incorrectly attributed to Anais Nin)

"Pursue your dreams not because you're immune to heartbreak, but because your real life, your whole life, is worth getting your heart broken a few thousand times."

~Martha Beck, American sociologist & author,
The Willingness Factor: Learn to Avoid Avoidance

"If one advances confidently in the direction of one's dreams, and endeavors to live the life which one has imagined, one will meet with a success unexpected in common hours."

~Henry David Thoreau, American essayist & writer,
Walden, or Life In the Woods

"Whoever is happy will make others happy too. He who has courage and faith will never perish in misery."

~Anne Frank, German diarist,
The Diary of a Young Girl

"Sometimes courage is the quiet voice at the end of the day saying, I will try again tomorrow."

~Mary Anne Radmacher, American artist & writer

"Courage is like a muscle. We strengthen it with use."

~Ruth Gordon, American actress & playwright

"Courage is resistance to fear, mastery of fear -- not absence of fear."

~Mark Twain, American humorist & author

"Trusting in yourself, not what you accomplish is the key to success."

~Deepak Chopra, Indian-American author,
Spiritual Solutions

"Life shrinks or expands in proportion to one's courage."

~Anais Nin, French writer

"Courage is the most important of all virtues, because without courage you can't practice any other virtue consistently. You can practice any virtue erratically, but nothing consistently without courage."

~ Maya Angelou, American poet & author

"Many of our fears are tissue paper thin, and a single courageous step would carry us clear through them."

~Brendan Frances Behan, Irish writer & poet

"Courage, it would seem, is nothing less than the power to overcome danger, misfortune, fear, injustice, while continuing to affirm inwardly that life with all its sorrows is good; that everything is meaningful even if in a sense beyond our understanding; and that there is always tomorrow."

~Dorothy Thompson,
American journalist & radio broadcaster

"If you've lost focus, just sit down and be still. Take the idea and rock it to and fro. Keep some of it and throw some away and it will renew itself. You need do no more."

~Dr. Clarissa Pinkola Estés,
American psychoanalyst & writer,
Women Who Run with the Wolves

"Creativity requires the courage to let go of certainties."

~Erich Fromm, German social psychologist,
author of The Art of Loving

"I learned that courage was not the absence of fear, but the triumph over it. The brave man is not he who does not feel afraid, but he who conquers that fear."

~Nelson Mandela,
President of South Africa & author,
Long Walk to Freedom

"Courage is not simply one of the virtues but the form of every virtue at the testing point."

~C. S. Lewis, British author,
The Screwtape Letters

"The opposite of courage is not so much fear as it is conformity."

~Dr. Wayne Dyer, American philosopher & author

"There has never been, and never will be, anyone who sees, thinks, or responds exactly the way you do. Whether you're revolutionizing physics or making a quilt, you must display your differences to make a difference."

~Martha Beck, American sociologist & author

"I can be changed by what happens to me, but I refuse to be reduced by it."

~ Maya Angelou, American poet & author

TIME

One day, I woke up to discover that my kids were grown and gone. It was a shock. How had I not noticed so much time passing? Wasn't it only a few months ago that I waited on the front steps for them to return home from their first day of school?

Sometimes weeks and months seemed endless, like the years of braces, music lessons, and the sullen teens. I yearned for the days of no more children to accommodate, teach, prod and cart hither and yon. When I arrived at that place, I felt quite different than I expected! I felt sad and lost.

As I began to reflect on this seemingly sudden shift in my worldview, I was forced to step back and really look at why I felt the way I did. As the dust settled it was clear to that I had gone through my life not really paying attention to the fullness of the moment. Focused on the demands of my children and our family business, I was locked in a state of "what's next-ness".

Consciously or unconsciously, we make one tiny decision after another that determines not only what happens, but how we experience our life. Behind the day to day demands and decisions, we choose in every moment what we think about! Most of us, particularly when we are young don't recognize that we have this choice, but we do.

In every moment we can choose to dwell in the past, think about what's coming, or place all our attention in the present moment.

I spent years striving toward one elusive goal after another. I spent endless hours thinking about this new business or that, this new home improvement project or that, worrying about some perceived problem my child had or another, fretting about how I had contributed to the problem and what I could do about it. Granted, these concerns are worth our time and attention, but only if we spend enough time in the present moment. How much is enough is an individual choice. We will know by the quality and texture of our lives.

When we are anxious and worried, it's a clear signal that we are living in a state of "what's next-ness" or ruminating on all that went from in the past.

When I watched my children walk through the door into the adult world on their own, I cried. Shortly after my father died and I cried again. Then, my mother died. Everything that held my life together while I was living in the future was dissolving, and while I was future living, I wasn't creating a life for myself that would stand the test of time.

It felt like I had blinked, and my life was over. The end loomed large, and the emptiness inside began filling up with panic and despair. Time. It really wasn't endless.

Eventually, I came to see that it wasn't the clock that needed adjusting, it was my underlying attitude and approach to life that had brought me to this reckoning. It was time to make significant changes on the inside, starting with my well entrenched habit of dwelling in the past and/or the future. NOW was where I needed to be.

Rediscovering a healthier relationship with time doesn't happen overnight. For me, it required a significant personal and spiritual unearthing that took many years to come to fruition and is ever evolving. But, this journey led me back to my soul-self and anchored me there, ultimately leading to a more joyful and meaningful existence.

Learning to live more fully in the present began for me when I started noticing how often my thoughts wandered into the future or sunk into the past. Then the practice began. When I noticed my thoughts straying too long in either direction, I pulled them back into the present. Early on my past/future thoughts were fueled by anxiety as I had not yet built up a secure foundation within myself. During those times, putting my attention in the present was often as simple as focusing on a single small object, such as the arm of the chair I was sitting in. I would study the texture, the feel, the color and try to take in every detail of the fabric. (This is a common mindfulness practice used to treat extreme anxiety and PTSD.)

This practice broke the spell in that moment and over time broke the hold my wandering mind had on my life.

Midlife and the awareness that "time waits for no one" is a perfect wake up call that reminds us to stop obsessing about what is yet to be and/or what has gone before.

We are exactly where we need to be. This moment is all that matters and all we really have. Today is not the first day of the rest of your life. It is the only day. Live it fully.

REFLECT on TIME:

How much time do you spend thinking about the past and/or future? What feelings are associated with these thoughts? What might you be missing in the present while your attention is elsewhere?

QUOTES ON TIME

"Whomever it is you were born to be, whatever your soul was coded to accomplish, whatever lessons you were born to learn, now is the time to get serious and get going."
~Marianne Williamson, American author
The Age of Miracles: Embracing the New Midlife

"Both young children and old people have a lot of time on their hands. That's probably why they get along so well."
~Jonathan Carroll, American author

"The great thing about getting older is that you don't lose all the other ages you've been."
~Madeleine L'Engle, American author

"If you start a day without a clear plan about how you're going to spend your attention, you'll end up wasting most of it."
~Martha Beck, American sociologist & author of
Finding Your Own North Star

". . . if we take care of the moments, the years will take care of themselves."
~Maria Edgeworth, Anglo-Irish author,
Moral Tales for Young People

"Time does not change us. It just unfolds us."
~Max Frisch, Swiss architect & writer,
Sketchbook

"Yesterday's the past, tomorrow's the future, but today is a gift. That's why it's called the present."

~ Bil Keane, American cartoonist,
Family Circle

"Don't spend time beating on a wall, hoping to transform it into a door."

~ Coco Chanel, French fashion designer

"Time is the coin of your life. It is the only coin you have, and only you can determine how it will be spent. Be careful lest you let other people spend it for you."

~Carl Sandburg, American journalist & poet,
at his 85th birthday party

"While you might be feeling a bit depressed that you are no longer young, you're ecstatic that you're no longer clueless."

~Marianne Williamson, American author,
The Age of Miracles: Embracing the New Midlife

"An unhurried sense of time is in itself a form of wealth."

~Bonnie Friedman, American writer,
in the New York Times

"The only reason for time is so that everything doesn't happen at once. "

~ Albert Einstein, German theoretical physicist

"The future is something which everyone reaches at the rate of 60 minutes an hour, whatever he does, whoever he is."

~C. S. Lewis, British author,
The Screwtape Letters

"I must govern the clock, not be governed by it."

~Golda Meir, former Prime Minister of Israel

"Empty time is a powerful medicine that can make us more joyful and resilient, but it's strangely hard to swallow."

~Martha Beck, American sociologist & author,
"Making Time for Nothing"

"The secret of health for both mind and body is not to mourn the past, worry about the future, or anticipate troubles, but to live in the present moment wisely and earnestly."

from The Teaching of Buddha
translated from the Japanese

"Yesterday is gone. Tomorrow has not yet come. We have only today. Let us begin."

~St. Mother Teresa, Albanian Roman Catholic nun
& missionary in Calcutta, India

"You must live in the present, launch yourself on every wave, find your eternity in each moment."

~Henry David Thoreau, American essayist & writer,
Journal

"Don't let the fear of the time it will take to accomplish something stand in the way of your doing it. The time will pass anyway; we might just as well put that passing time to the best possible use."

~ Earl Nightingale,
American radio personality, writer, speaker, & author

"Nobody sees a flower really; it is so small. We haven't time, and to see takes time - like to have a friend takes time."

~ Georgia O'Keeffe, American artist

"At the end of your life, you will never regret not having passed one more test, not winning one more verdict or not closing one more deal. You will regret time not spent with a husband, a friend, a child, or a parent."

~ Barbara Bush, former First Lady

"How did it get so late so soon?"

~Theodor Geisel, aka Dr. Seuss,
American author & artist,
Pocket Poems

DECISION

The demands on our time tend to increase steadily with each passing year, until at midlife they reach an uncomfortable crescendo. We have more and more choices to make about how we spend our time.

Each decision we make, or do not make, shapes the person we have become and will become in the future. For better or worse, our lives reflect our choices.

When we stand ready to decide our next step, our choices are not always clear. When my mother was in her nineties and living alone I was faced with a decision that would alter my life. Should I move her in to live with my family? I had one son in college and one in high school. We had a home-based business and life was complicated. To compound matters, my mother and I did not always have an easy relationship and it would add significant stress to my already overstressed life.

Still, I knew in my heart that it was the best option for her. The question became, should I do what is best for me, or for her? Was there any room for a compromise?

At times, we must choose to risk more than we feel capable of risking. Sometimes we must say no. It is not always clear which choice is the best. We may have an inkling of direction, but in many of major life decisions, the water is just murky enough to give us pause. Whether we forge ahead with gusto or plod along agonizing over each step, the course is the same. Choices must be made: simple or complex, insignificant or monumental.

As in the case of moving Mom in my home, there are often no clear, right-or-wrong choices, just shades of gray. We think and ruminate and weigh and measure with the best of our rational minds. Perhaps if we stopped straining to see the but closed our eyes and listened instead, we might hear the voice of our heart, where the truth is most often found.

When we view the world only through the lens of our rational mind, the opinion of others may block out our own solution.

Our true and most meaningful direction will come only when we listen to the quiet voice within us, the one we too often bury as we focus on externals. It is my experience that Truth speaks more often in feelings and nuances than in bold statements. We must be utterly still to hear it.

Build your dreams upon the foundation of sincere desire, not on the subtle expectations of others that you may have come to believe are your own.

REFLECT on DECISION

How do you make decisions?

_____
_____
_____
_____
_____
_____
_____
_____
_____

Do you have a major decision to make? What is it?

_____
_____
_____
_____

View your time and energy as currency. The amount is finite. Think about how you would like to spend this currency in your life.

_____
_____
_____
_____
_____
_____
_____
_____
_____
_____
_____

QUOTES ON DECISION

"It is in your moments of decision that your destiny is shaped."

~Anthony Robbins,
American author & motivational speaker

"Begin making choices based on what makes you feel freer and happier, rather than how you think an ideal life should look. It's the process of feeling our way toward happiness, not the realizing of some Platonic ideal, that creates our best lives."

~Martha Beck, American sociologist & author,
"How to Escape Your Rat Race"

"Nothing ever goes away until it has taught us what we need to know."

~Pema Chodron,
American Tibetan Buddhist & author,
When Things Fall Apart: Heart Advice
for Difficult Times

"When we let go of the constant attempts to solve the content of our lives and attend to the important process of how we treat ourselves and each other, we have a real chance for peace of mind."

~ Thomas Rutledge,
American psychotherapist & author

"Once you make a decision, the universe conspires to make it happen."

~Paul Coelho, Brazilian writer,
The Alchemist

"Perfectionism is a state of perpetual victimization. Decision-making is a state of constant learning."

~Thomas Rutledge,
American psychotherapist & author

"One night, I lay awake for hours, just terrified. When the dawn finally came up - the comfortable blue sky, the familiar world returning - I could think of no other way to express my relief than through poetry. I made a decision there and then that it was what I wanted to do. Every time I pulled a wishbone, it was what I asked for."

~ Alice Oswald, British poet

"Life isn't about waiting for the storm to pass, it's about learning how to dance in the rain."

~Vivien Greene,
Rhodesian author & antique dollhouse expert

"The self is not something ready-made, but something in continuous formation through choice of action."

~John Dewey, American author,
Democracy and Education

"The most difficult thing is the decision to act, the rest is merely tenacity. The fears are paper tigers. You can do anything you decide to do. You can act to change and control your life; and the procedure, the process is its own reward."

~ Amelia Earhart, American aviator & author

"I am not a product of my circumstances. I am a product of my decisions."

~Stephen Covey, American educator & author

"If you limit your choices only to what seems possible or reasonable . . . you disconnect yourself from what you truly want, and all that is left is a compromise."

~Robert Fritz, American author & composer,
The Path of Least Resistance

"The hardest thing about the road not taken is that you never know where it might have led."

~Lisa Wingate, American author,
A Month of Summer

"Always go with the choice that scares you the most, because that's the one that is going to require the most from you."

~Caroline Myss, American teacher & author

"The most difficult thing is the decision to act, the rest is merely tenacity. The fears are paper tigers. You can do anything you decide to do. You can act to change and control your life; and the procedure, the process is its own reward."

~ Amelia Earhart, American aviator & author

"Authenticity is a collection of choices that we have to make every day. It's about the choice to show up and be real. The choice to be honest. The choice to let our true selves be seen."

~Brené Brown, American researcher & author,
The Gifts of Imperfection: Let go of Who You Think
You're Supposed to Be and Embrace Who You Are

"Be miserable. Or motivate yourself. Whatever has to be done, it's always your choice."

Dr. Wayne Dyer, American philosopher & author

"You can't make decisions based on fear and the possibility of what might happen."

~ Michelle Obama,
former First Lady, lawyer & writer

"On an important decision one rarely has 100% of the information needed for a good decision no matter how much one spends or how long one waits. And, if one waits too long, he has a different problem and has to start all over. This is the terrible dilemma of the hesitant decision maker."

~ Robert K. Greenleaf, author,
The Servant as Leader

"The truth is that many people set rules to keep from making decisions."

~Mike Krzyzewski, author & basketball coach,
author Leading with the Heart

SILENCE

Rainy days can be depressing. Occasionally, however, they evoke a calm reverence for quiet and solitude, a perfect opportunity to hunker down and enjoy the quiet.

One morning I awoke to just such a day. This day I recognized it for the rare gift that it was and decided to embrace it. I indulged my moody, reflective nature and snuggled under the cover of introspection.

My fury companion decided however, that he preferred to walk through puddles, and I reluctantly acquiesced.

So, I, sweatshirted and hooded myself and with leash in hand we ventured forth into the pouring spring rain. As we walked, my resistance to walking began to slip away and a more awake and vibrant energy moved in. Before I knew it, I felt invigorated. The cool, moist air filled my lungs and my mind picked up pace to match my quickening steps.

Uninhibited, all controls off, I felt my thoughts begin to settle into a comfortable kind of sorting, like clearing the clutter on a computer desktop. . . this goes here, that goes there, this can be discarded, that I want to keep.

We came into rhythm, my brain and me, and it felt amazing! I rarely give myself permission to take my hands off the controls of my thoughts. I more often "focus" on one problem or another, one after another. On this day, walking in the rain, my thoughts did what they needed to do, and was liberating, a task that needed to be done.

I often write about the benefits of a "quiet time." Today I learned the value of a different kind of quiet . . . one that consists of stepping back and letting my hands off the controls enough to allow my thoughts to go where they needed to go; to disconnect from purposeful, guided brain activity, including a self-imposed quiet time. Sometimes the brain just needs to do its own thing!

I wonder how children who are subjected to mandated "quiet time" might react to the concept of "think time" instead of what is often perceived by them as forced and uncomfortable confinement. Would they be more cooperative and less resistant to stopping their activities if given something on which to focus their attention? Would this not be preferable, and more natural, than the arduous task of shutting down their eager little minds and bodies entirely, a task inordinately difficult for most? Might teachers use this opportunity to instruct their students on how to tune in to their inner voice, the voice of their hearts, the magic of their imagination? It seems to me it would be a beneficial life lesson that might lay the very groundwork for their lives as adults in a crazy world. I imagine that children might find this a fascinating and interesting activity while achieving the same beneficial results as a quiet rest. In many cases I'm sure many children would fall asleep more easily.

For weary adults, a long walk in the rain without electronic attachments is a perfect way to create an opportunity for "think time." We cannot always break away from the worry and planning and active thinking of our minds. But we can create space and time for the possibility that our thoughts might enjoy an opportunity to find their own path. This is often best done through trickery such as a walk in the rain.

REFLECT on SILENCE

How do you feel about silence? Does it frighten you? Draw you in? What about it attracts you? What do you fear?

_____

_____

_____

_____

_____

_____

_____

_____

_____

_____

_____

_____

_____

_____

How much time do you spend in silence each day? Each week?

_____

_____

_____

_____

_____

_____

_____

_____

Change does not happen overnight. It's a practice. Here's one to get you started.

A DAILY DOSE OF PEACE

Begin today to connect to you and to the creative spirit that lives within you. Step by step, moment by moment, be still and rest in the beautiful creation that is you.

Rest in Quiet.

Quiet is a soothing balm for some while it can be a terrifying void for others. No matter where you are on the continuum, you are where you are supposed to be.

Just begin.

Add a small dose of quiet to your day, every day that you can. It might simply be a few minutes in the car after you've turned off the engine or while sitting on your porch in the sun after dinner. Find a time and a place to just breathe. Breathe in the stillness. Breathe in the clarity that quiet can provide. Connect with whatever it is that feels like the center of your being.

Build on this.

Add five minutes, or ten, until you are comfortable and connected with a place you know is you . . . a place where you can hear the still, small voice of your heart.

Rest in Beauty.

Take in the beauty around you. If there is none, create some by closing your eyes and using your imagination to create the most beautiful, warm, and loving place. you can imagine, where you are safe from all harm and have everything you need. Dwell on a beautiful flower, a masterful painting, a lyric in a poem, a melody that lifts your spirits. Absorb beauty in all its magnificence.

Replace the stress and the violence of the news with the lilt of Enya's melodies. Assemble the most wonderful photos you can find and place them where you will see them often. Whenever possible, seek beauty first. The beauty that touches you is within you. If you feel moved to create, create from the beauty that lives and breathes within you. The act of creation connects us to our deepest selves and the source of our being. It is the very core of the dreams we've yet to uncover.

Rest deeply, fully, completely. Stop the forward motion of your mind and body. Put aside that one-more-thing that you think you must do . . . and rest. Sleep, if that is what comes. Sit. Read. Listen. Turn down the volume of your thoughts in any way you can. Busy your hands with needlework if you must, but make sure that what you do with your hands is something that creates beauty.

If you can, go away from your day-to-day

demands to a place that nurtures your soul—the beach, a mountainside cabin, a library, or a bookstore. For an hour, a day, or a week, go wherever is possible, whatever the deep fatigue and disconnect within you requires. You will know. Turn off the demands and rest.

QUOTES ON SILENCE

"The best way to break through any barrier is to access a point of perfect stillness at the center of your being, a self deeper than your senses or your mind."
~*Martha Beck, American sociologist & author,*
The Joy Diet: 10 Daily Practices for a Happier Life

"Take as much stuff off your plate as possible, so you can focus on doing what's important, and doing it well."
~*Leo Babauta, American author,*
Zen to Done

"Peace comes from within. Do not seek it without."
~*attributed to Marcus Aurelius*
in <u>Country Life</u> *magazine, 1908*

"True silence is the rest of the mind; it is to the spirit what sleep is to the body, nourishment and refreshment."
~*William Penn, English philosophy, businessman*
& founder, the English North American colony
of the Province of Pennsylvania

"You do not need to leave your room. Remain sitting at your table and listen. Do not even listen, simply wait, be quiet, still and solitary. The world will freely offer itself to you to be unmasked, it has no choice, it will roll in ecstasy at your feet."
~*Franz Kafka, German-Bohemian writer*

"Quiet minds cannot be perplexed or frightened, but go on in fortune or misfortune at their own private pace, like a clock during a thunderstorm."

~Robert Louis Stevenson, Scottish author,
"La Fere of Cursed Memory"

"The quieter you become, the more you can hear."

~Baba Ram Dass,
American author & spiritual teacher

"There is a place in you where there is perfect peace. There is a place in you where nothing is impossible. There is a place in you where the strength of God abides."

~Helen Schucman & William Thetford,
American authors, A Course in Miracles, "Lesson 41"

"Silence is a doorway into the heart of reality; to cultivate a silent heart is to discover your deepest truth."

~Nan C. Merrill, American author
Lumen Christi . . . Holy Wisdom: Journey to Awakening

"When you rest in quietness and your image of yourself fades, and your image of the world fades, and your ideas of others fade, what's left? A brightness, a radiant emptiness that is simply what you are."

~Adyashanti, American author & spiritual teacher

Sitting quietly, doing nothing, spring comes and the grass grows by itself.

~Zenrin Poem

"Traditionally we are taught, and instinctively we long, to give where it is needed—and immediately. Eternally; woman spills herself away in driblets to the thirsty, seldom being allowed the time, the quiet, the peace, to let the pitcher fill up to the brim."

~Anne Morrow Lindbergh, American author,
Gift from the Sea

"The question we need to ask ourselves is whether there is any place we can stand in ourselves where we can look at all that's happening around us without freaking out, where we can be quiet enough to hear our predicament, and where we can begin to find ways of acting that are at least not contributing to further destabilization."

~Baba Ram Dass,
American author & spiritual teacher

"I've begun to realize that you can listen to silence and learn from it. It has a quality and a dimension all its own."

~ Chaim Potok, American author & rabbi

"We need to find God, and he cannot be found in noise and restlessness. God is the friend of silence. See how nature - trees, flowers, grass- grows in silence; see the stars, the moon and the sun, how they move in silence... We need silence to be able to touch souls."

~ St. Mother Teresa, Albanian Roman Catholic nun
& missionary in Calcutta, India

"Learn to get in touch with the silence within yourself and know that everything in life has purpose. There are no mistakes, no coincidences, all events are blessings given to us to learn from."

~ *Dr. Elisabeth Kubler-Ross,*
Swiss-American psychiatrist & author,
On Death and Dying

"If you don't die of thirst, there are blessings in the desert. You can be pulled into limitlessness, which we all yearn for, or you can do the beauty of minutiae, the scrimshaw of tiny and precise. The sky is your ocean, and the crystal silence will uplift you like great gospel music, or Neil Young."

~ *Anne Lamott, American author & writer*

FORGIVENESS

Forgiveness does not come easily to most of us. As years, experiences, hurts, and mishaps pile up, finding our way through the debris to forgiveness can be very challenging. As time passes, we lose sight of where one hurt ends and another begins. Unfinished business permeates our lives and our days often become a confusing landscape of yesterday's disappointments and today's concerns. In this mystifying place, we find ourselves navigating land mines of anger and hurt, unable to set our sights on what really matters.

Without forgiveness -- especially forgiveness of ourselves -- the world turns dark. Our pain and discomfort, however, is an ever-present reminder to take care of our unfinished business.

Forgiveness is not about relinquishing control accepting the unacceptable. It is something quite different. Our pain instructs us to look at ourselves and others in a new light – and take a more objective perspective.

Wounds inflicted on us by others carry no power over us without our help and attention. The first step to finding forgiveness is to turn away from the other and turn toward ourselves. We must look within at how we are perpetuating the pain by our unwillingness to do the work to let it go. What is this hurt we carry really about? Where does our responsibility for healing it lie?

Before forgiveness can take place, we must first heal ourselves. This is done by exposing our wounds to light of love and acceptance. . . our love and acceptance. As we turn our attention away from our wounding and embrace self-healing practices of love and acceptance, in time we will come to know forgiveness.

First, love yourself. Care for yourself. Heal yourself. If you do not hold hatred in your heart, then you will be free to love again. Through this process you will learn to forgive.

REFLECT on FORGIVENESS

Is there a hurt that you have not forgiven? Name it.

_____

_____

_____

_____

_____

_____

_____

_____

_____

Do you believe you are responsible for this hurt in some way? Are you?

_____

_____

_____

_____

_____

_____

Think of a hurt child. How would you comfort her? Do this for yourself.

_____

_____

_____

_____

_____

_____

_____

QUOTES ON FORGIVENESS

"How does one know if she has forgiven? You tend to feel sorrow over the circumstance instead of rage, you tend to feel sorry for the person rather than angry with him. You tend to have nothing left to say about it all."

~Dr. Clarissa Pinkola Estés,
American psychoanalyst & writer,
Women Who Run with the Wolves

"To forgive is to set a prisoner free and discover that the prisoner was you."

~Lewis B. Smedes, American author,
Forgive and Forget: Healing the Hurts
We Don't Deserve

"If you let go of the past and move with your dreams, it will always be enough."

~Mike Dooley, American author,
Notes from the Universe: New Perspectives
from an Old Friend

"Forgiveness can be more than an act of the moment; it can be a way of life."

~Whitley Strieber, American writer

"The heart of a mother is a deep abyss at the bottom of which you will always find forgiveness."

~Honore de Balzac, French writerg6c;

"Always forgive your enemies—nothing annoys them so much."

~*Oscar Wilde, Irish playwright & author*

Forgiveness is the fragrance the violet sheds on the heel that has crushed it.

~*Unknown*

"When you hold resentment toward another, you are bound to that person or condition by an emotional link that is stronger than steel. Forgiveness is the only way to dissolve that link and get free."

~*Catherine Ponder, American minister & author,*
Joy is an Inside Job: 12 Timeless Secrets for Abundance,
Radiant Health, and Lifelong Happiness

"Life is an adventure in forgiveness."

~*Norman Cousins, American political journalist*
& writer, in the Saturday Review

"Forgiveness is a virtue of the brave."

~*Indira Gandhi, former Prime Minister of India*

"You can't forgive without loving. And I don't mean sentimentality. I don't mean mush. I mean having enough courage to stand up and say, 'I forgive. I'm finished with it."

~ *Maya Angelou, American poet & author*

"Forgiveness is like faith. You have to keep reviving it."

~*Mason Cooley,*
American academic & aphorist

Return to the centre of your heart; not your past.

~Unknown

"Darkness cannot drive out darkness; only light can do that. Hate cannot drive out hate; only love can do that."

~ Dr. Martin Luther King, Jr., American Baptist Minister
& Civil Rights Movement activist,
"Nobel Peace Prize Acceptance Speech," 1964

"Forgiveness is the final form of love."

~ Reinhold Niebuhr, American theologian,
author Moral Man, Immoral Society

"When you hold resentment toward another, you are bound to that person or condition by an emotional link that is stronger than steel. Forgiveness is the only way to dissolve that link and get free."

~ Catherine Ponder, American minister & author

"When another person makes you suffer, it is because he suffers deeply within himself, and his suffering is spilling over. He does not need punishment; he needs help. That's the message he is sending."

~ Thich Nhat Hanh, Vietnamese Buddhist Monk

"Sincere forgiveness isn't colored with expectations that the other person apologizes or change. Don't worry whether or not they finally understand you. Love them and release them. Life feeds back truth to people in its own way and time."

~ Sara Paddison, American author

"The first step in forgiveness is the willingness to forgive."

~ Marianne Williamson, American author

"When a deep injury is done to us, we never heal until we forgive."

~ Nelson Mandela, former President of South Africa

"Getting over a painful experience is much like crossing monkey bars. You have to let go at some point in order to move forward."

~ C.S. Lewis, British novelist & poet

"Holding on to anger is like drinking poison and expecting the other person to die."

~ Emmet Fox, American author,
summarized from a passage in his book,
The Sermon on the Mount

"How people treat you is their karma; how you react is yours."

~ Dr. Wayne Dyer, American philosopher & author

HOPE

Most of us give life our best effort. We work hard to make the best decisions and choose the right path. Still things go wrong. Then, we chastise ourselves and promise we'll be smarter and wiser and more careful the next time. Sometimes we are, and sometimes we step right back into the same minefield. In the process we may begin to lose hope of every "getting it right". We lose confidence in ourselves and in life.

A psychological experiment created by Cornell University psychologists offers us a clue as to why we may not trust ourselves. In this study, called the "Visual Cliff," a group of babies who could crawl, but not yet walk, were placed on a glass bottom platform. Part of the platform was on top of solid ground and part was extended out over open space. As the babies crawled forward, they crossed onto the glass floor that was transparent. As you may know, we are born with an instinctive fear of falling. This research experiment was designed to assess the babies' responses in a frightening situation.

Across the room, the mothers of the babies were divided into two groups. One group contained mothers who were told to smile encouragingly at their children as they approached the open space. The other group of mothers was asked to frown and look fearful when their baby looked at them. Neither group was to speak.

In all instances, the babies whose mothers

looked at them with encouragement and smiles continued out onto the transparent glass flooring despite the normal fear of falling. The other babies, who looked at the faces of frightened, worried mothers, did not venture forth.

From infancy, our parents' responses to us either reinforced our fears or set us free. Those of us whose mothers were fearful received a multitude of signals that taught us to be cautious. This has made it difficult for us to move into dangerous territory with ease and confidence.

This does not mean, however, that overly cautious people are fatally flawed. What it does mean is that extra courage and work is needed to venture forth. Being aware of our fear is the first step to overcoming it. Each time we name our fear, we take one more step in taking control of it.

Our fears may take a variety of forms. They may even give us false messages about what we think we want to do. We may mistake the voice of fear for our inner voice. Fear is very powerful mask.

How then do we determine whether we are haring fear or inner guidance? All we need to do is ask ourselves one question, "Does this choice say, 'yes to life, or no?" Fear closes doors; it does not open them. Fear keeps us stuck. Saying *yes* moves us forward. Even if we realize in time that the step was not the right one. We learned something about ourselves and will always grow as a result.

To develop a hopeful heart, fear must be relegated to its proper place. It has its value. It warns us of danger, but all danger does not carry the same weight.

Choosing to hope over living in fear keeps our lives moving forward. Hope grows us. Fear freezes us. Each of us find a balance between the two.

REFLECT on HOPE

What do you hope for?

_____

_____

_____

_____

_____

_____

_____

_____

_____

Tune in to your body. When you feel hope where in your body do you feel it? Can you describe it?

_____

_____

_____

_____

_____

_____

_____

_____

_____

What do you fear? Where do you feel it in your body?

_____

_____

_____

_____

_____

QUOTES ON HOPE

"You gain strength, courage, and confidence by every experience in which you really stop to look fear in the face. You must do the thing which you think you cannot do."

~Eleanor Roosevelt, former First Lady & author,
You Learn by Living

"Hope is both the earliest and the most indispensable virtue inherent in the state of being alive. If life is to be sustained hope must remain, even where confidence is wounded, trust impaired."

~Erik H. Erikson, German-American developmental
psychologist & author,
Insight and Responsibility

"Far away there in the sunshine are my highest aspirations. I may not reach them, but I can look up and see their beauty, believe in them, and try to follow where they lead."

~Louisa May Alcott, American writer

"You may say I'm a dreamer, but I'm not the only one. I hope someday you'll join us. And the world will live as one."

~John Lennon, British musician & lyricist,
from the song, "Imagine"

"If you only walk on sunny days you'll never reach your destination."

~Paulo Coelho, Brazilian novelist

"The simple act of hopeful thinking can get you out of your fear zone and into your appreciation zone -- a habit that can replace anxiety with happy participation."

~Martha Beck, American sociologist & author,
"Have You Created Your Magic List Yet?"

"Hope is the thing with feathers
that perches in the soul –
and sings the tunes without the words –
and never stops at all . . ."

~Emily Dickinson, American poet,
"Hope is the thing with feathers"

"When one door closes another door opens; but we so often look so long and so regretfully upon the closed door, that we do not see the ones which open for us."

~Alexander Graham Bell, American inventor

"The great challenge of adulthood is holding on to your idealism after you lose your innocence."

~Bruce Springsteen,
American singer, musician & author

"Expect to have hope rekindled. Expect your prayers to be answered in wondrous ways. The dry seasons in life do not last. The spring rains will come again."

~Sarah Ban Breathnach, American author,
Simple Abundance

"Keep some room in your heart for the unimaginable."

~ Mary Oliver, American poet

"Listen to the mustn'ts child.
Listen to the don'ts.
Listen to the shouldn'ts, the impossibles, the won'ts.
Listen to the never haves, then listen close to me . . .
Anything can happen, child.
Anything can be."

~Shel Silverstein, American poet,
"Where the Sidewalk Ends"

If I keep a green bough in my heart, the singing bird will come.

~ Proverb

"Everything that is done in the world is done by hope."

~Martin Luther,
German founder of the Lutheran Church

"Hope
Smiles from the threshold of the year to come,
Whispering 'it will be happier' . . ."

~Alfred, Lord Tennyson, English poet,
"The Foresters"

"Hope is sweet-minded and sweet-eyed. It draws pictures; it weaves fancies; it fills the future with delight."

~Henry Ward Beecher, American Congregationalist
clergyman, Proverbs from Plymouth Pulpit

"Start by doing what is necessary, then do what is possible, and suddenly you are doing the impossible."

~St. Francis of Assisi, Italian Roman Catholic friar

"The very least you can do in your life is to figure out what you hope for. And the most you can do is live inside that hope."

~*Barbara Kingsolver, American author,*
Animal Dreams

"May your choices reflect your hopes, not your fears."

~ *Nelson Mandela, former President of South Africa*

"There is some good in this world, and it's worth fighting for."

— *J.R.R. Tolkien, British author,*
The Two Towers

PURPOSE

Childhood is a magical time. The innocent see life differently. A child has enormous curiosity, endless good will, eternal hope, and complete faith in life. The years, though, may whittle away our innocence and undermine our confidence in life. Yet I believe that the gifts we given to us at birth are still with us and last far beyond childhood. They have simply gone underground for safekeeping until such time that we can once again appreciate them and put them to effective use.

As a child, I lived in the magnificent state of Maine. It was pure heaven for a kid like me. Building snow forts and sucking on icicles were among my favorite pastimes in winter . . . catching polliwogs and climbing to the top of an enormous rock with my best friend for a picnic in the woods were my summertime delights. It was home to me, and I loved it.

I didn't brood on unpleasant things. What I faced as a child would seem monumental to me as an adult. Health issues, loneliness, the drudgery of day-to-day life in school, and the difficulty of being painfully shy. I didn't lose myself to self-pity or pay too much attention to the sadness I felt. Instead, I found peace when I could in the woods and streams of unsullied nature. I drew enormous yellow suns on the whitest paper I could find when winter grew dark and long. I created warmth where I could and allowed it to shine down on me.

Children are amazingly resilient creatures. It behooves each of us to get reacquainted with the one that still lives inside of us. Take a few moments to roust that innocence from its long winter of hibernation, and you may just discover remnants of your authentic self. The hope and joy that existed in our own hears and comforted us then, may be just what we need today to face life's challenges.

As a child, I knew the face of God, though She did not have a name. I trusted implicitly the outstretched arms of protection that held me securely when I rested in the hollow of an enormous tree. I soaked up the comforting aroma of the woodsy smell of nature. A force of hope fueled and inspired me as I watched day after day an enormous icicle grow on the corner of our little house. One day it reached the ground.

I absorbed the charity and benevolence of nature, mesmerized by the drip, drip, drip of maple syrup as it flowed from the little tube my dad inserted into our maple tree. It was easy to rest in the unending peace that comforted me as I lay in my mother's lap on Sunday mornings. As I listened with my whole being to the echoes of reverence and the sweet scent of flickering candles I was lulled to sleep. I knew God then. Only I have changed.

REFLECT on PURPOSE

Recall what you loved to do as a child? What brought you pleasure? What books do you enjoy reading? Can you describe this child?

_____

_____

_____

_____

_____

_____

_____

_____

_____

_____

_____

_____

Do you still take time to do any of these things? What could you do today to bring this child into your life now? Perhaps you can not do the same thing, but a different version of it. For instance, your love for climbing trees may be a love of walking in the woods now.

_____

_____

_____

_____

_____

_____

_____

_____

QUOTES ON PURPOSE

"Your purpose is that something you express in everything you do. It's your reason for existence."
~Jonathan Mead,
American job coach & writer

"Dreams pass into the reality of action.
From the actions stems the dream again;
and this interdependence produces
the highest form of living."
~Anais Nin, French author

"I have come to the conclusion that as much as we may think we want life to be easy and to be fed like babies— whether that's by food companies or the entertainment industry— we all have a desire for something more."
~Natalie M. Holmes, American author

"The world needs dreamers and the world needs doers. But above all, the world needs dreamers who do."
~Sarah Ban Breathnach, American author

"If you believe you can, you probably can. If you believe you won't, you most assuredly won't.
Belief is the ignition switch that gets you off the launching pad."
~Denis Waitley,
American motivational speaker & writer

"None of your pain has been pointless and no part of your life has been wasted."
~Martha Beck, American sociologist & author,
The Four-Day Win: End Your Diet War
and Achieve Thinner Peace

"How wonderful it is that nobody need wait a single moment before starting to improve the world."
~Anne Frank, German diarist,
The Diary of a Young Girl

"Too far, and too much, are excuses we have all overcome when what we needed to do mattered more than the excuse we held!"
~Dõv Baron, Canadian author

Our lives begin to end the day we become silent about things that matter.
~ Dr. Martin Luther King, Jr., American Baptist Minister
& Civil Rights Movement activist,
from a 1965 sermon

"It is good to have an end to journey towards; but it is the journey that matters, in the end."
~Ursula K. Le Guin, American author,
The Left Hand of Darkness

"The need to find meaning . . . is as real as the need for trust and for love, for relations with other human beings."
~Margaret Mead, American anthropologist & writer

"Passion is energy. Feel the power that comes from focusing on what excites you."

~Oprah Winfrey,
American media host, actor & producer

"Pursue some path, however narrow and crooked, in which you can walk with love and reverence."

~Henry David Thoreau,
American essayist & writer,
Journal

"People often say that motivation doesn't last. Well neither does bathing — that's why we recommend it daily."

~Zig Ziglar,
American motivational speaker & author

"If you don't know where you're going, any road will get you there."

~George Harrison, English singer & songwriter,
"Any Road"

"Life has no meaning in itself, but only in the meaning we give it. Like the clay in the artist's hands, we may convert it into a divine form or merely into a vessel of temporary utility."

~Lama Anagarika Govinda, Buddhist teacher & poet

"Find out who you are and do it on purpose."

~Dolly Parton,
American singer & songwriter

"Your beliefs become your thoughts.
Your thoughts become your words.
Your words become your actions.
Your actions become your habits.
Your habits become your values.
Your values become your destiny."

~Mahatma Gandhi, leader of India's
Independence Movement

CREATIVITY

Oscar Wilde wrote that "life imitates art more than art imitates life." I see the evidence of this everywhere. Each day that we live, we experience emotions, gather insights, reflect and tuck away memories, knowledge, and understanding. We use these tools as an artist would her palate of colors and her brushes to create a masterpiece. Moment by moment, bit by bit we apply the lines, shapes, and hues that paint our days. With each stroke of the brush we bring our canvas to life.

As we create, we have a certain amount of freedom to choose what we paint. We can choose whether or not we fashion an impression of our inner truth or something entirely different. Day by day, we make the decisions and take the actions that lead us to a finished piece. When we step back and study what we have created, we ask ourselves if we like what we see. Have we created an authentic masterpiece or a clumsy knock off? Should we toss this canvas, and start a new one?

In life we have an opportunity to begin again, to change course, to abandon one project or ideation and start anew. As we add experience and knowledge to our palette we see fresh possibilities that fire our imagination and stir our creative juices. We may rush to complete the canvas we are working on or abandon it entirely and begin again.

Midlife gives us an opportunity to step back and

assess what we have created. Do we like what we see, or have the colors grown stale, the impression muddy? Are we struggling to blow fresh life into a canvas that has been overworked, or have we lost interest in our original idea?

A new perspective is stirring. We are changing inside and out. We feel unsettled and uncertain. A sense of urgency is building as we recognize that more than half of our life is over. Age-old questions arise: "What is the meaning of life?" or more precisely "What is the meaning of my life?" "What is my purpose? Have I fulfilled it?"

We no sooner ask these questions than one more question arises. How do these answers to these questions inform my choices for the remainder of my life?

Change of any kind creates a spark that can ignite our creativity. Now, at this point, it is the perfect time to pull out a fresh canvas and begin again. We have learned so much! We are skillful artists of life despite our practical success or failure. We are no longer apprentices. We are more than ready to bring our experience to bear on our most exquisite creation thus far.

This is our chance to create a life that is even more in tune with the vision of our heart, one that more accurately resembles the depth of our spirit and the complexities of our soul. Some of our attempts will be good and worthwhile, and some will belong in the trash. But we are quicker now to discern the good from the bad, the true from the false. We are not ready to give up. Each stroke we make, each color we choose now will more closely resemble the color and hue of our souls.

Life, like art, is fluid. It changes color with the change of light. A brush stroke adds dimension and depth; it also changes the perspective and appearance. A slight change in perspective allows us to turn a painful experience into a gift of healing for another.

As we age, we must take advantage of our experienced artist's eye, working carefully and cleverly to use our gifts as we are inspired to do. There are as many new canvases as there are squares on the calendar of our lives. We are endowed with the opportunity to fill each one with all the movement and color we have to offer, as continue each day to work toward our final exhibition.

Tune in to your creativity. It will lead you to the deepest expression of you and bring you face to face with your authentic self. Isn't this what life is all about?

REFLECT on CREATIVITY

What inspires you? When do you lose yourself in what you're doing? Think outside of the box. You may be a painter, or writer, or dancer, but your creativity may be sparked by something quite different.

_____

_____

_____

_____

_____

_____

_____

_____

What do you lay awake nights thinking about? Even if it's worry, that is where your creative energy is going.

_____

_____

_____

_____

_____

Name three creative ideas you've had this week. Do you follow their lead?

_____

_____

_____

_____

_____

QUOTES ON CREATIVITY

"Confusion is the welcome mat at
the door of creativity."
>~Michael J. Gelb, American author & public speaker

"Thought is the sculptor who can create
the person you want to be."
>~Henry David Thoreau, American essayist & writer

"People often say that this or that person has not yet
found himself. But the self is not something one finds;
it is something one creates."
>~Dr. Thomas Szasz, American psychiatry professor,
>The Second Sin

"There is within each of us the possibility of
magnificence. Every moment is an opportunity to
make it manifest."
>~Marianne Williamson, American author

"The very motion of our life is towards happiness."
>~Dalai Lama XIV, spiritual leader of Tibet,
>The Art of Happiness in a Troubled World

"Happiness is not an ideal of reason, but of
imagination."
>~Immanuel Kant, German philosopher & writer,
>Fundamental Principles of the Metaphysics of Ethics

"Live out of your imagination, not your history."
>~Stephen Covey, American author
>7 Habits of Highly Effective People

"Imagination is more important than knowledge. Knowledge is limited. Imagination encircles the world."

~*Albert Einstein, German physicist & author,*
Saturday Evening Post interview, 1929

"The power is in you. The answer is in you. And you are the answer to all your searches: you are the goal. You are the answer. It's never outside."

~*Eckhart Tolle, Canadian author &*
spiritual teacher, The Power of Now

"Creativity comes from trust. Trust your instincts."

~*Rita Mae Brown, American author*

"Creativity is a shape changer. One moment it takes this form, the next that. It is like a dazzling spirit who appears to us all, yet is hard to describe for no one agrees on what they saw in that brilliant flash."

~*Dr. Clarissa Pinkola Estés,*
American psychoanalyst & writer,
The Gift of Story: A Wise Tale
About What Is Enough

"Within every woman there is a wild and natural creature, a powerful force, filled with good instincts, passionate creativity, and ageless knowing."

~*Dr. Clarissa Pinkola Estés,*
American psychoanalyst & writer,
Women Who Run with Wolves

And those who were seen dancing were thought to be insane by those who could not hear the music.

~Unknown

"Music is the language of the spirit. It opens the secret of life bringing peace, abolishing strife."

~Kahlil Gibran, Lebanese-American writer & poet

"When we neglect the artist in ourselves, there is a kind of mourning that goes on under the surface of our busy lives."

~Pat Schneider, American author,
Writing Alone and with Others

"Every artist dips his brush in his own soul, and paints his own nature into his pictures."

~Henry Ward Beecher,
American Congregationalist clergyman & author,
Norwood: Or, Village Life in New England

"Art is a personal act of courage, something one human does that creates change in another."

~Seth Godin, American author,
Linchpin: Are You Indispensable?

"Anxiety is part of creativity, the need to get something out, the need to be rid of something or to get in touch with something within."

~David Duchovny, Canadian actor & writer

"A hunch is creativity trying to tell you something."

~Frank Capra, Italian-American film producer

"Courage is the price that life exacts for granting peace."

~*Amelia Earhart, aviation pioneer & author*

ATTITUDE

Of all the lessons I've learned in the past decade, the most valuable has been recognizing the value of gratitude. For the first fifty years of my life I was driven by destination thinking, the relentless need to get someplace "better". I did not take the time to appreciate my accomplishments, but simply moved on to the next goal.

I seldom rested long enough to see the abundance life provided me without my conscious effort. One of the gifts of aging is our willingness to slow down. Sometimes it is forced upon us by illness or decreased energy. If we do not resist the slowing down, we may see its value. When we give up the chase, our attention is freed to come into present time where we may discover that we have much to be grateful for.

On the suggestion of a good friend, I began to keep a gratitude journal. At first, I could only come up with three or four three things that I was grateful for each night before I went to sleep.   Soon, however, it became easier and easier. My nightly list grew to five or six items each day, and one I didn't write in my journal was how grateful I was for my new, more positive perspective.

As with all good intentions that we attempt but have yet become habit, this practice fell by the wayside. In time, my positive approach to life disintegrated to old habits of thought. My focus shifted to what was wrong with my life instead of what was right with it. That is until I was reminded again, this time by a quote on Facebook, to begin again to practice gratitude. As I did, my attitude improved.

Changing our attitude can be as simple as changing the direction of our thoughts. Thoughts go through our minds all day long. When we take a few moments periodically to tune into the specifics of our thoughts, particularly the ones we are only vaguely aware of, we will discover mind chatter that is anything but helpful! The quickest way to create a new attitude, is to catch self-defeating thoughts and turn them into something more constructive.

Our attitude about any situation is our habit of thought about it. It can be positive or negative. It is our choice.

REFLECT on ATTITUDE

Take a few moments a couple of times a day and tune into your thoughts. Go behind your feelings to the thoughts that propel them. Write them down these thoughts.

_____

_____

_____

_____

Consider the nature of these thoughts. Are they positive or negative? Are you beating up on yourself? Are you being critical of everyone and everything? Are you wallowing in self-pity? Are you worrying yourself sick about something that has yet to happen?

_____

_____

_____

_____

_____

Take each thought and write the opposite. Consider what there is to be grateful for in that situation.

_____

_____

_____

_____

_____

_____

QUOTES ON ATTITUDE

"When you judge another, you do not define them, you define yourself."

~Dr. Wayne Dyer, American philosopher & author

"The only disability in life is a bad attitude."

~Scott Hamilton,
American Olympic athlete & commentator

"If you have not slept, or if you have slept, or if you have headache, or sciatica, or leprosy, or thunder-stroke, I beseech you, by all angels, to hold your peace, and not pollute the morning."

~Ralph Waldo Emerson
American philosopher & essayist,
from the essay "Conduct of Life"

"The secret of staying young is to live honestly, eat slowly, and lie about your age."

~Lucille Ball, American actor & comedian

"Think of yourself as a problem solver not a collection of problems."

~Thomas Rutledge,
American psychotherapist & author

"Act as if what you do makes a difference. It does."

~William James, psychologist & philosopher,
author The Will to Believe, Human Immortality

"If you don't like something, change it. If you can't change it, change your attitude."

~Maya Angelou, American poet & author

"A single gentle rain makes the grass
many shades greener. So our prospects
brighten on the influx of better thoughts."
~Henry David Thoreau, American essayist & writer,
<u>Walden, or Life In the Woods</u>

"Being powerful is like being a lady. If you have to tell
people you are, you aren't."
~Margaret Thatcher, former Prime Minister
of the United Kingdom

"Whenever you become intensely focused on
changing someone else's behavior, you might want to
check what part of your own business you're
avoiding."
~Martha Beck, American sociologist & author

If you want to fly, you have to give up the thing that
weighs you down.
~Toni Morrison, author
paraphrase from her novel, Song of Solomon

When there is no enemy within, the enemies outside
cannot hurt you.
Sir Winston Churchill, former British Prime Minister &
author,
possibly adapted from an African proverb

". . . we cannot become what we want to be by
remaining what we are."
~Max DePree, American businessman & author,
Leadership Is an Art

"A positive attitude may not solve all of your problems, but it will annoy enough people to make it worth the effort."

~Herman Oliver Albright,
German artist & philosopher

SUCCESS

The young have a unique advantage. They tend to be more willing to believe that anything is possible. Even in my darkest days as a teen and young adult, I believed that if I worked hard enough and did all the right things, I would achieve my heart's desire. If I didn't let my foot off the accelerate I would, sooner or later, "arrive". I knew it would not be perfect, but it would be good enough.

Little did I know that I would be trapped by a mindset, passed down from generation to generation. It would keep me bound and guided by forces I could not see. Driven by a combination of habit, ego, and an immature idea of love and caring, I plowed through the first half of my life as if my days on earth were endless. It is crystal-clear to me, now that I have really "come of age," that life is not what it seems when we are young!

When I woke up from a life that now seems like a bad dream, I was nearly paralyzed by the awareness that, despite 50 years of effort and determination, I was no nearer my original destination than I had been 30 years earlier. I felt as though I had wasted my life. I had given it away, keeping little for myself.

My immediate response was to announce to myself and to anyone who would listen, "I'm done doing for everyone else. I'm done living my life for my children, my parents, my husband, my friends, my animals, my job! It's time for me!" Those who bothered to listen undoubtedly heard the panic in my voice and heard what I was really saying: "I'm running out of time! I need to pick up the pace!"

It has been almost ten years since this turning point. I still battle some of the false beliefs that pre-programmed my life, but the battle is fought with a little more wisdom and compassion. One of my most important lessons can be summed up in this quote by Lyanla Vanzant: "The only way to get what you really want is to let go of what you don't want." We cling tenaciously to so many things in life, many of which have no real value in the overall scheme of things. These "things" keep us trapped, bound, and unhappy, whether they are material possessions, jobs, ideas, or people.

The "letting go" is not always simple or easy, and it isn't a "once and done" kind of thing. To find a life of joy and meaning, we must let go repeatedly. It is the only way to keep moving forward toward the life we were meant to live. The minute we begin to cling to something that does not bring joy and meaning to our lives, we can be certain that we are going away from our true selves instead of toward them. What drives us then is not passion, but fear or insecurity.

When we cling tenaciously to what we are doing, we use up the emotional and practical space we need to keep for something better. Sometimes, we heap another layer on top, trying to kill the pain and discomfort of living our wrong choices. Perhaps we douse ourselves in alcohol, material things, vacations, a new romance, or a myriad of other escape tools. By filling our days with placebos, from the hedonistic to quasi-spiritual, we simply muffle our fears. We accomplish only temporary escape from a life of true joy and inner peace.

Gradually, day by day, we can learn to let go of those things that do not make us happy. In the empty space that remains, we are then free to fill it with something that brings us joy, or perhaps just leave it empty. Empty space is a powerful place where magic happens if we do not run from it. Turning toward it, allowing ourselves to sit with the discomfort, beautiful new surprises will arise from within us. Let go of the desire to have all of the answers today.

REFLECT on SUCCESS

What does success mean to you?

_____

_____

_____

_____

_____

_____

_____

Has your idea of success changed over the years? How?

_____

_____

_____

_____

_____

_____

_____

Name something in your life that doesn't serve you but takes up your time. Are you willing to let it go?

_____

_____

_____

_____

_____

_____

_____

_____

_____

QUOTES ON SUCCESS

"The only way to get what you really want is to let go of what you don't want."

~Iyanla Vanzant,
American author, speaker & lawyer

"Empty pockets never held anyone back. Only empty heads and empty hearts can do that."

~Dr. Norman Vincent Peale,
American minister & author,
Enthusiasm Makes the Difference

"The difference between success and failure isn't the absence of fear but the determination to pursue your heart's desires no matter how scared you are."

~Martha Beck, American sociologist & author

"I'd rather have roses on my table, than diamonds on my neck."

~Emma Goldman,
Lithuanian political activist & author

"Belief in oneself is one of the most important bricks in building any successful venture."

~Lydia M. Child, American activist

"Success is liking yourself, liking what you do and liking how you do it."

~Maya Angelou, American poet & author

"When you dance, your purpose is not to get to a certain place on the floor. It's to enjoy each step along the way."

~Dr. Wayne Dyer, American philosopher & author

"It doesn't matter how long we may have been stuck in a sense of our limitations. If we go into a darkened room and turn on the light, it doesn't matter if the room has been dark for a day, a week, or ten thousand years—we turn on the light and it is illuminated."

~Sharon Salzberg,
American author & Buddhist teacher

"Obstacles are those frightful things you see when you take your eye off the target."

~Henry Ford, American industrialist

"The ladder of success is best climbed by stepping on the rungs of opportunity."

~Ayn Rand, Russian-American novelist & writer

"It is hard to fail, but it is worse never to have tried to succeed."

~Theodore Roosevelt,
26th President of the United States

Success is not the key to happiness. Happiness is the key to success. If you love what you are doing, you will be successful.

~Unknown

"The first step toward achieving excellence is imperfection."

~Martha Beck, American sociologist & author

"Failure is success in progress."

~ Albert Einstein, German theoretical physicist

"Find somebody to be successful for. Raise their hopes. Think of their needs."

~Barack Obama, 44th President of the United States

"Living our life deeply and with happiness, having time to care for our loved ones – this is another kind of success, another kind of power, and it is much more important."

~Thich Nhat Hanh, Vietnamese Buddhist monk

"The real test is not whether you avoid this failure, because you won't. It's whether you let it harden or shame you into inaction, or whether you learn from it; whether you choose to persevere."

~Barack Obama, 44th President of the United States

AUTHENTICITY

I've been an avid proponent of being "real" for as long as I can remember. In high school, my best friend and I often discussed what that meant to us. We didn't like "phonies" – people who pretended to be something they weren't. But how did we know? And were we able to be "real" just because we understood the concept?

At that point in my life, and long after, my desire for an authentic life continued as I made choices that went against the grain of cultural norms. I was rebellious in the sixties, I tried to conform in the seventies, convincing myself I could be authentic in a business suit. In the eighties I chose to forgo a career to be a stay-at-home Mom. My deep held belief that children need their parents, especially in the early years has never faded. I didn't much like the job, but it was mine and I knew it.

And yet, I couldn't own this part of my authentic self. I felt guilty when people asked me, "what do you do?", and I had to answer, "I'm a stay at home Mom." The culture's eye told me I was not living up to expectations.

In the 90's my husband and I went into business for ourselves. Yes, I was still rebellious, and so was he! Driven to build a business from the ground up I tossed aside a major portion of my true self. I put it on the shelf beside my philosophy and theology books and focused on raising my children and making us rich.

At the turn of the century midlife descended, along with aging and dying parents, my children leaving home, 9/11 and a downturn in the economy followed by a downturn in our business. My health began to disintegrate, and my authentic self was no where to be found!

What I learned through the unearthing of my authentic self is that it is very difficult to live authentically when we are unaware of the hidden forces that are driving us.

To be authentic is to align our outsides with our insides. In other words, who I am on the inside must be the same as who I am on the outside. Looking at our Facebook feed, it is easy to discern that most people do not show up as their authentic selves in this place. They mask, pretend, display, brag, deflect and any number of conscious and unconscious tricks to protect themselves. Why do they do this? Because being authentic means being vulnerable and being vulnerable puts us right smack in the cross hairs of being hurt.

The two most crucial practices necessary to develop an authentic life, are a) understand how your past influences your present, and b) dare to show up and practice what you preach.

Feeling free to be exactly who we are does seem to get easier with age. The desire to please others decreases while the desire to please oneself increases. This is as it should be. We've given our understanding and our compassion to our children, our jobs, our spouses and friends, and we've asked little in return. Now it is time to learn how to ask for as well as to give.

We are now free to call back our forgotten dreams, to stir up the muse who lay sleeping while we toiled with practical matters. It is time to dance with our spirit and create something new from all that we have experienced. Our authentic self is not lost; it has just been biding its time in patient repose waiting for us to be ready to bloom.

The wise woman finds her way into communion with her muse, takes hold of her creative core and spins a tale of beauty and truth with ever-increasing ease. This is the gift she will give to the world, and it is her responsibility to reveal the truth to others through the way she lives her life. Each woman has a unique melody, a tune, and an opportunity to sing her own song. The world needs real. The world needs authentic. The world needs us.

REFLECT on AUTHENTICITY

What does being authentic mean to you?

_____

_____

_____

_____

Name one positive and one negative way your upbringing shaped your attitude?

_____

_____

_____

_____

_____

_____

Is this attitude or belief one you'd like to keep? If not, what belief would be more in line with your authentic self?

_____

_____

_____

_____

_____

_____

_____

_____

_____

_____

_____

QUOTES ON AUTHENTICITY

"Today it's time for authentic "truth or dare." Dare yourself to believe in your creativity, wherever it may lead you. Trust that where it leads is exactly where you're supposed to be."

~Sarah Ban Breathnach, American author,
Simple Abundance

"Boredom is the root of all evil — the despairing refusal to be oneself."

~Sören Kierkegaard, Danish philosopher & poet

"Always be a first-rate version of yourself, instead of a second-rate version of somebody else."

~Judy Garland, American singer & actor

"It took me a long time not to judge myself through someone else's eyes."

~Sally Field, American actor

"Be yourself. Everyone else is already taken."

~Oscar Wilde, Irish playwright, humorist & author

"What is uttered from the heart alone,
will win the heart of others to your own."

~Johann Wolfgang von Goethe,
German writer & statesman

"The privilege of a lifetime is being who you are."

~Joseph Campbell,
American writer & mythologist

"Constantly measuring ourselves against others sours and shortens our lives, robbing us of the very things we think it will bring: prosperity, love, inner peace, the knowledge that we're good enough."

~Martha Beck, American sociologist & author,
"You vs Her: How to Stop the Mind Games
You Just Can't Win!"

"Best advice I ever heard: 'Be who you are and say what you feel because people who mind don't matter and people who matter don't mind.'"

~Theodor Geisel, aka Dr. Seuss,
American author & artist

"At fifty, the madwoman in the attic breaks loose, stomps down the stairs, and sets fire to the house. She won't be imprisoned anymore."

~Erica Jong, American satirist & writer,
Fear of Fifty: A Midlife Memoir

"Ask yourself right now, "What's my own nature if I have no outside forces telling me who or what I should be? "Then work at living one day in complete harmony with your own nature, ignoring pressures to be otherwise."

~Dr. Wayne Dyer, American philosopher & author

"That inner voice has both gentleness and clarity. So, to get to authenticity, you really keep going down to the bone, to the honesty, and the inevitability of something."

~Meredith Monk,
American singer & composer

"Before speaking, consult your inner-truth barometer, and resist the temptation to tell people only what they want to hear."

~Dr. Wayne Dyer,
American philosopher & author

"Beneath, around, even within the cacophonous chaos of your life disintegrating, something infinitely powerful and surpassingly sweet is whispering to you."

~Martha Beck,
American sociologist & author,
The Joy Diet: 10 Daily Practices for a Happier Life

"Once you become Real you can't become unreal again. It lasts for always."

~Margery Williams, English-American author,
The Velveteen Rabbit

"Transcending labels that you've placed on yourself or that others have placed upon you opens you up to the opportunity of soaring in the now in any way you desire."

~Dr. Wayne Dyer,
American philosopher & author

"Say, do, and be what you would if no one else were looking. It will be scary at first, but if you persist, there will come that liberating moment when you'll feel yourself sailing straight through your life's most inhibiting barriers without even feeling a bump."

~Martha Beck, American sociologist & author,
"How to Cure Self-consciousness"

FRIENDSHIP

Friends are a gift. They are not earned, begged, borrowed, or stolen. Real friends that is. They are angels that the heavens blow into our lives when we need them the most. At least that has been my experience,

It's not that we can lay back and idly wait for the universe to provide a friend – although sometimes it does. But, if we truly want someone special to be a part of our lives, we must go to work and prepare the soil.

First, we must carry on as if we are worthy of the gift we are anticipating. We must turn our attention away from what we do not have to what we have – ourselves. Next, we must become our own best friend! Focusing on the inner work of building our self-esteem and showing up in the world as exactly who we are is the best way to attract friends that we want.

In other words, we must do what we love, and friendship will bloom. If we like to travel, we'll probably enjoy others who like to travel. So, travel we must! Venture outside of our comfort zone and pushing the edges of comfort is a good exercise for all of us. When we live our life fully, the angels know when we are ready to accept the gift of friendship.

Real friendships cannot be rushed, manufactured, or cajoled. They just are. And, they take time, attention and care, like anything of value.

A soul friend may only come along once or twice in a lifetime. But one true soul friend, a person who sees our true self, is enough A soul friend is someone who not only accepts us but elevates our perspective of ourselves is a special gift indeed. To be "seen" by someone is a treasure.

A soul-friend also gives us the very things we didn't know we needed, and an opportunity to feel ourselves in ways previously undefinable. A soul friend teaches us how to love ourselves as they love us. Conversation with a soul friend is as natural as the breeze, and laughter comes easily.

Friendship of all types teaches us about trust, boundaries, forgiveness and acceptance. All friendships take attention and work. I

In tough times, a devoted friend will walk beside us offering a shoulder to cry on, a listening ear, or a hand to hold. They will celebrate our successes, hurt with us in our sorrow, and walk beside us as we search for direction. They encourage us when we've lost hope and never, ever let us give up. They will always see us truer than we see ourselves, both in our gifts and our shortcomings -- they always, always see us as magnificent no matter how often we fall. They offer a helping hand and help brush us off when we're ready to get back on the road. A friend such as this just might be life's greatest blessing.

REFLECT on FRIENDSHIP

What does friendship mean to you?

_____

_____

_____

_____

_____

_____

_____

_____

_____

_____

_____

_____

_____

_____

_____

_____

_____

_____

_____

_____

_____

_____

_____

_____

_____

QUOTES ON FRIENDSHIP

"God gave us our relatives; thank God we can choose our friends."

Ethel Watts Mumford, American author

"Those who love you are not fooled by mistakes you have made or dark images you hold about yourself. They remember your beauty when you feel ugly; your wholeness when you are broken; your innocence when you feel guilty; and your purpose when you are confused."

Alan Cohen, American author

"Remember, we all stumble, every one of us. That's why it's a comfort to go hand in hand."

Emily Kimbrough, American author & journalist

"When we are dreaming alone it is only a dream. When we are dreaming with others, it is the beginning of reality."

Dom Helder Camara,
Brazilian Catholic Archbishop

"People come into your life for a reason, a season or a lifetime. When you figure out which it is, you will know exactly what to do."

~Chris Moon-Willems,
American social work consultant

"Conflict cannot survive without your participation."

~Dr. Wayne Dyer,
American philosopher & author

"Surround yourself with high-energy people. Choose to be in close proximity to people who are empowering, who appeal to your sense of connection to intention, who see the greatness in you, who feel connected to God, and who live a life that gives evidence that Spirit has found celebration through them."

~Dr. Wayne Dyer, American philosopher and author

"A little Consideration, a little Thought for Others, makes all the difference."

~Dr. Leslie Parrott, American author,
You Matter More Than You Think

"You cannot truly listen to anyone and do anything else at the same time."

~M. Scott Peck, American psychiatrist & author

"If you don't risk anything, you risk even more."

~Erica Jong, American author,
Becoming Light: Poems New and Selected

"A friend is a loved one who awakens your life in order to free the wild possibilities within you."

~John O'Donohue, Irish author,
Anam Cara: A Book of Celtic Wisdom

Don't walk in front of me; I may not follow. Don't walk behind me; I may not lead. Just walk beside me and be my friend.

~Unknown

"Honest disagreement is often a good sign of progress."

~Mahatma Gandhi, leader of India's
Independence Movement

"A single rose can be my garden . . . a single friend, my world."

~Leo Buscaglia,
American author & motivational speaker

"The best method to break out of solitary confinement is to seek to understand others, and help them understand you."

~Martha Beck, American sociologist & author,
"When You Feel Lonely"

"One of the oldest human needs is having someone to wonder where you are when you don't come home at night."

~Margaret Mead, cultural anthropologist & author

"A real friend is one who walks in when the rest of the world walks out."

~Walter Winchell,
American newspaper & radio commentator

"You're imperfect, and you're wired for struggle, but you are worthy of love and belonging."

~Dr. Brené Brown, Researcher and Author

"No person is your friend who demands your silence or denies your right to grow."

~ Alice Walker, Author of The Color Purple

"No one can develop freely in this world and find a full life without feeling understood by at least one person."

~Paul Tournier, Swiss physician & author,
To Understand Each Other: Classic Wisdom
on Marriage

"Nobody needs a smile more than the one that cannot smile to others."

~Dalai Lama XIV, spiritual leader of Tibet

"Each friend represents a world in us, a world possibly not born until they arrive, and it is only by this meeting that a new world is born."
~ Anaïs Nin, The Diary of Anaïs Nin, Vol. 1: 1931-1934

JOY

Joy. It's not a giggle, or a laugh, or a thing gone exactly right. It's not the warm feeling of love when a small child smiles up at you. It's not the hope you feel upon waking up on a sunny day when the world feels just right. It's no one thing, but someone all of them. Life when it's sprinkled with moments, a little here, a little there that causes one to feel giddy for no apparent reason.

Joy is something most of us try to capture and hold on to, like if we tried hard enough we could possess it for life. What happens, however, when we do this is that we squeeze the life out of the joy that is right in front of us! Joy is fleeting, yet ever-present. It's not meant to be held or contained and it may appear as an open, held crescendo or yet a mere whisper.

Joy arises when we least expect it; in that moment we allow our worries to take a back seat and our fears to go on vacation; and in those rare moments when we give up our need to control life and ourselves. Chase it though we might (and often do), it will elude us when we grasp for it. It is not a thing to be possessed.

Joy defies description, restriction, or conscription. It will not be quantified, controlled, or directed. It just is. We may open ourselves to the possibility of it, but we cannot direct its path.

We know joy when we experience it, and our only obligation to it is to breathe it in and say, "Thank you."

REFLECT on JOY

How would you describe joy?

_____

_____

_____

_____

_____

_____

_____

_____

_____

_____

_____

_____

_____

_____

Describe a time when you experienced joy?

_____

_____

_____

_____

_____

_____

_____

_____

_____

QUOTES ON JOY

"Life may not be the party we hoped for, but while we're here we should dance."
> ~*Jeanne C. Stein, American urban fantasy author,*
> <u>*Blood Drive*</u>

"When we create harmony in our minds and hearts, we will find it in our lives. The inner creates the outer. Always."
> ~*Louise L. Hay, American motivational author*

"There are exactly as many special occasions in life as we choose to celebrate."
> ~*Robert Brault, American free-lance writer*

"Don't postpone joy until you have learned all of your lessons. Joy is your lesson."
> ~*Alan Cohen, American author*

Don't cry because it's over; smile because it happened.
> ~*attributed to Theodor Geisel, aka Dr. Seuss, American*
> *author & artist*

"The most wasted of all days is one without laughter."
> ~*E.E. Cummings, American artist & poet*

"Certainly, work is not always required . . . there is such a thing as sacred idleness -- the cultivation of which is now fearfully neglected."
> ~*George MacDonald,*
> *Scottish author & Christian minister*

"When you do things from your soul, you feel a river moving in you, a joy."

~Rumi, Persian poet & scholar,
"Moving Water"

"I don't think of all the misery, but of the beauty that still remains."

~Anne Frank, German diarist,
The Diary of a Young Girl

"Sometimes your joy is the source of your smile, but sometimes your smile can be the source of your joy."
~Thích Nhất Hạnh, Vietnamese Buddhist monk

"The beating heart of the universe is holy joy."
~Martin Buber, Jewish theologian,
author I and Thou

"The gloom of the world is but a shadow; behind it, yet within our reach, is Joy."

~Fra Giovanni Giocondo,
Italian friar and architect,
in "Letter to a Friend" 1513

"Joyfulness keeps the heart and face young. A good laugh makes us better friends with ourselves and everyone around us."
~Orison Swett Marden, American author

"Music... will help dissolve your perplexities and purify your character and sensibilities, and in time of care and sorrow, will keep a fountain of joy alive in you."
~ Dietrich Bonhoeffer, German pastor & theologian

"Some of you say, "Joy is greater than sorrow," and others say, "Nay, sorrow is the greater." But I say unto you, they are inseparable. Together they come, and when one sits alone with you at your board, remember that the other is asleep upon your bed."

~ *Kahlil Gibran, Lebanese-American writer & poet,*
The Prophet

"There is not one blade of grass, there is no color in this world that is not intended to make us rejoice."

~ *John Calvin, French pastor & theologian*

"Life itself is the proper binge."

~*Julia Child, American chef & author*

LOVE

We have all been wounded. Many of us bear the deep scars of a less-than-perfect childhood. Perhaps our parents didn't, or couldn't, love us the way we needed to be loved -- the way all children deserve to be loved. Or maybe another person or experience left a mark on our psyche and heart so painful that we put in place cleverly devised layers of protection to keep us safe from future harm.

Self-protection has its benefits, but it also has its dangers. The longer we live and the more we have loved and lost, the more likely we are to be weighed down by our own cleverness. We may even feel smug about our ability to "carry on" despite life's eventualities. Or, we may be able to turn the other cheek with increasing ease. Wisdom allows us to do this to some extent, but we must take a closer look as we may, in fact, simply be numb.

If you look into the eyes of an innocent child who was loved into awakening, you will see the wide-eyed goodness of easy trust, acceptance, and love . . . a love that flows freely without boundaries or limitations or expectations. That was us. . . once.

We cannot go back to the point of perfect innocence. But if we dare, we can choose to stare down our fears, open our hearts and love again. This, of course, is not an effortless process, but it begins the moment we decide to step into vulnerability. And, it is a decision.

We can decide to let go of the past, and more importantly it's control over our hearts and emotions. We have reached the point in our lives when we know we can survive hurt and loss. We have done it so many times before! We may know the pain that open, trusting, unsuspecting love can bring, but we also know its deep, abiding joy and life-giving power. If we do not know it, it's time to step into its power to heal.

We owe it to ourselves and to those who are in our lives, to keep taking the risk to love and allow ourselves to be loved. It is the only authentic way to know the fullness of life. After all, as Bette Midler sings in "The Rose," "It is the heart afraid of breaking that never learns to dance."

REFLECT on LOVE

Are you afraid of love? Do you remember a time when you were not?

_____

_____

_____

_____

_____

_____

_____

_____

_____

_____

_____

_____

_____

_____

Brene Brown in her book "Daring Greatly" says this about vulnerability: "Courage starts with showing up and letting ourselves be seen." What could you do today to show up and be seen?

_____

_____

_____

_____

_____

_____

_____

_____

_____

QUOTES ON LOVE

". . . in a person-to-person encounter, love listens. It is its first task to listen."
>*~Paul Tillich, author The Courage to Be*
>*German-American Christian existentialist philosopher*

"There are two ways of spreading light . . . to be the candle, or the mirror that reflects it."
>*~Edith Wharton, American writer & poet,*
>*from the poem "Vesalius in Zante. (1564)"*

"Wake at dawn with a winged heart and give thanks for another day of loving."
>*~Kahlil Gibran, Lebanese-American writer & poet,*
>*The Prophet*

"A hug is like a boomerang—you get it back right away."
>*~Bil Keane, American cartoonist,*
>*from The Family Circus*

"Love sometimes wants to do us a great favor: hold us upside down and shake all the nonsense out."
>*~Hafez of Shiraz, Persian poet*

"Let there be spaces in your togetherness and let the winds of heavens dance between you.
Love another but make not a bond of love.
Let it rather be a moving sea between the shores of your souls."
>*~Kahlil Gibran, Lebanese-American writer & poet, The*
>*Prophet*

"My life is an indivisible whole, and all my attitudes run into one another; and they all have their rise in my insatiable love for mankind."

~Mahatma Gandhi, leader of India's
Independence Movement

"You never lose by loving. You always lose by holding back."

~Dr. Barbara De Angelis,
American relationship consultant,
Chicken Soup for the Couple's Soul

If you love somebody, let them go, for if they return, they were always yours. And if they don't they never were.

~Unknown

"No one can give you anything—love, shame, self-esteem—until you give it to yourself. Today, give yourself good things."

~Martha Beck, American sociologist & author

"Being deeply loved by someone gives you strength, while loving someone deeply gives you courage."

~Laozi (also Lao-Tzu), Chinese Philosopher

"Being heard is so close to being loved that for the average person they are almost indistinguishable."

~Dr. David W. Augsburger,
American Anabaptist author

To the world you might be one person, but to one person you might be the world.

~Unknown

"Let passion be your muse. Let her guide and teach you to trust your instincts."

~*Sarah Ban Breathnach, American author,*
<u>Simple Abundance</u>

"Whoever said love is blind is dead wrong. Love is the only thing that lets us see each other with the remotest accuracy."

~*Martha Beck, American sociologist & author*

"It's so clear that you have to cherish everyone. I think that's what I get from these older black women, that every soul is to be cherished, that every flower is to bloom."

~*Alice Walker, African-American writer*

It is better to be hated for what you are than to be loved for what you are not.

~*André Gide,*
French author & Nobel Prize winner,
Autumn Leaves

"You don't love someone because they're perfect, you love them in spite of the fact that they're not."

~*Jodi Picoult, American author,*
My Sister's Keeper

"Let us love, since our heart is made for nothing else."

~*St. Therese of Lisieux, French Roman Catholic nun,*
from "Letter to her Cousin Marie Guerin"

"Love is not something we give or get; it is something that we nurture and grow, a connection that can only be cultivated between two people when it exists within each one of them – we can only love others as much as we love ourselves."

~ Brené Brown, <u>The Gifts of Imperfection</u>: Let Go of Who You Think You're Supposed to Be and Embrace Who You Are

"Love is what we were born with. Fear is what we learned here."

~Marianne Williamson, American author, "Born with Love"

HAPPINESS

We all have times when we feel stuck. Stuck in a job, a town, a state, a house, or even a climate that doesn't seem to resonate with our spirit. There may be a set of circumstances that seem beyond our control working against our creative energy. We may be stuck in a relationship, a lifestyle, or mired in habits and addictions we can't seem to break.

As we age, we may find that the future has become a less appealing place in which to dwell, so we begin to dwell in the past. We become obsessed with trying to unravel all of the hurts and disappointments we have experienced and to make sense of them. We try to "understand" ourselves, believing it will free us from our unhappiness.

Living in any place of "stuck-ness" can foster an underlying, and often unrelenting sense of frustration, anger, despair or hopelessness. We can't seem to see our way out; we can't find our way through; we can't even see what's right in front of us.

Breaking out of a pattern of "stuck-ness" requires letting go -- letting go of the goal, the dream, the elusive solution to your problem. Ultimately, this may mean letting go of the belief that obtaining whatever it is you are obsessed with is the only avenue to happiness and peace of mind. In reality, these things are a means of escaping, avoiding, or eluding what is right in front of you. You cannot become unstuck by focusing on something outside of yourself, because the stuck-ness lives within you.

Begin to break free by choosing to set your obsession on an imaginary shelf. Stop yourself from thinking about it; take a vacation from it. Select a period of time, a day, a week, a month, to give up working on this problem. Then take a deep, long breath and breathe in the fresh air of freedom, and enjoy the space you now have in your body, mind, and spirit.

Once an hour or once a day, think about or write down one thing you are grateful for. Make this a routine. If the obsession starts to rear its ugly head, replace it with a thought of something you appreciate in the here and now. Turn your attention to what is right in front of you. Listen. What do you hear? Breathe in. What do you smell? Relax your eyes and let your gaze fall where it will. What do you see? Focus on the smallest area you can and describe it to yourself. Experience it.

Letting go does not mean giving up. It does not mean abandoning your dreams. Letting go offers a way to gain perspective and to participate in a bigger reality. It opens space in your psyche and your soul for new and different solutions, for thoughts, ideas, and opportunities that were locked away from view. When we fight and struggle with reality, we work against ourselves. We become so invested in the outcome that we miss the more important things in life. Don't miss your life!

REFLECT on HAPPINESS

What do you believe is keeping you from being happy?

_____

_____

_____

_____

_____

_____

_____

_____

_____

_____

_____

What thoughts will you choose to let go?

_____

_____

_____

_____

_____

What are you grateful for today?

_____

_____

_____

_____

_____

QUOTES ON HAPPINESS

"The path to enlightenment is not a path at all, it's actually a metaphor for the time it takes for you to allow yourself to be happy with who you already are, where you're already at, and what you already have — no matter what."

~Mike Dooley, American inspirational author,
Notes from the Universe

"My life has no purpose, no direction, no aim, no meaning, and yet I'm happy. I can't figure it out. What am I doing right?"

~Snoopy, philosophical beagle,
from the Peanuts comic strip

"Happiness is when what you think, what you say and what you do are in harmony."

~Mahatma Gandhi, leader of India's
Independence Movement

"Your life follows your attention. Wherever you look, you end up going."

~Martha Beck, American sociologist & author

"We tend to forget that happiness doesn't come as a result of getting something we don't have, but rather of recognizing and appreciating what we do have."

~Frederick Keonig, German inventor

"If you smile when no one else is around, you really mean it."

~Andy Rooney, American radio & television writer

"It's a helluva start, being able to recognize what makes you happy."
>
> ~*Lucille Ball, American actor & comedian*

"To be kind to all, to like many and love a few, to be needed and wanted by those we love, is certainly the nearest we can come to happiness."
>
> ~*Mary Stuart, Queen of Scots 1542-1567*

"Happiness is something that comes into our lives through doors we don't even remember leaving open."
>
> ~*Rose Wilder Lane,*
> *American journalist & co-founder*
> *of the Libertarian party*

"You have to sniff out joy. Keep your nose to the joy trail."
>
> ~*Buffy Sainte-Marie,*
> *Native American singer & songwriter*

"Just let go. Let go of how you thought your life should be, and embrace the life that is trying to work its way into your consciousness."
>
> ~ *Caroline Myss, American teacher & author*

"Learning to live in the present moment is part of the path of joy."
>
> ~*Sarah Ban Breathnach, American author*

Happiness is something you decide on ahead of time.
>
> ~*Unknown*

"Happiness is not something you postpone for the future; it is something you design for the present."

~ Jim Rohn, American author & motivational speaker

"The power for creating a better future is contained in the present moment: You create a good future by creating a good present."

~ Eckhart Tolle, Canadian author &
spiritual teacher

"Real generosity toward the future lies in giving all to the present."

~ Albert Camus, French philosopher, author, and
journalist.

GRATITUDE

Gratitude is the cornerstone of happiness. Without gratitude, we cannot experience either happiness or inner peace. They go hand in hand. Cultivating a habit of gratitude enhances our ability to turn our attention from life's sadness and disappointment to what is good and valuable in our lives.

A "practice" is the best way to replace old thoughts and behaviors with new ones. Thus, when we choose to think less of our pain, sorrow and disappointment, and more of our blessings and good fortune, life changes hue. We are lifted up, body, mind and spirit.

It is difficult to hold two thoughts at one time. Replacing a negative thought with a positive one is an effective tool for dispelling all sorts of tiresome mental habits that do not serve us.

Taking a few minutes each day to list five things, large or small, for which we are grateful is a perfect start. As Sarah Ban Breathnach describes in her book Simple Abundance, expressing gratitude produces a smile without effort. We feel lighter, and more hopeful. This has been my experience.

It is important to remember that a grateful heart does not just "happen". We cannot wait for it to suddenly appear. Unless we help it along, by noticing the positive things about our day and life,

Begin today to practice gratitude. I have no

doubt you will notice the difference almost immediately. I did.

REFLECT on GRATITUDE

What are you grateful for?

_____

_____

_____

_____

_____

_____

_____

_____

_____

_____

_____

What are the details of your gratitude practice? When, where and how will you hold yourself accountable?

_____

_____

_____

_____

_____

_____

_____

_____

_____

_____

_____

_____

_____

QUOTES ON GRATITUDE

I had no shoes and complained,
until I met a man who had no feet.
~Saadi Shirazi, Persian poet,
paraphrased from his book, Gulistan

"Wake at dawn with a winged heart and give thanks
for another day of loving."
~Kahlil Gibran, Lebanese-American writer,
The Prophet

"One looks back with appreciation to the brilliant
teachers, but with gratitude to those who touched our
human feelings. The curriculum is so much necessary
raw material, but warmth is the vital element for the
growing plant and for the soul of the child."
~Carl Jung, Swiss psychiatrist & writer,
The Development of Personality

"As you breathe in cherish yourself. As you breathe
out cherish all beings."
~Dalai Lama XIV, spiritual leader of Tibet

"Gratitude unlocks the fullness of life. It turns what
we have into enough, and more. It turns denial into
acceptance, chaos to order, confusion to clarity. It can
turn a meal into a feast, a house into a home, a stranger
into a friend. Gratitude makes sense of our past,
brings peace for today and creates a vision for
tomorrow."
~Melody Beattie, American self-help author

"Gratitude changes the pangs of memory into a tranquil joy."
~Dietrich Bonhoeffer, German philosopher& writer,
"Separation from Those We Love"

"In ordinary life we hardly realize that we receive a great deal more than we give, and that it is only with gratitude that life becomes rich."
~Dietrich Bonhoeffer, German philosopher & writer,
Letters and Papers from Prison

"You can be thankful no matter how little you think you have, and with that gratitude comes personal power, responsibility, and the quiet confidence that what you have is all you need."
~Sue Ann Crockett, American writer

"Today expect something good to happen to you no matter what occurred yesterday. Realize the past no longer holds you captive. It can only continue to hurt you if you hold to it. Let the past go. A simply abundant world awaits."
~ Sarah Ban Breathnach, Simple Abundance: A Daybook of Comfort and Joy

"At times, our own light goes out and is rekindled by a spark from another person. Each of us has cause to think with deep gratitude of those who have lighted the flame within us."
~ Albert Schweitzer, OM was an Alsatian theologian, organist, writer, humanitarian, philosopher, and physician.

"Gratitude is the fairest blossom which springs from the soul."

> ~ *Henry Ward Beecher, American Congregationalist clergyman, social reformer, and speaker, known for his support of the abolition of slavery,*

"Joy is the simplest form of gratitude."

> ~ *Karl Barth, Swiss Reformed theologian who is often regarded as the greatest Protestant theologian of the twentieth century*

"No one who achieves success does so without the help of others. The wise and confident acknowledge this help with gratitude."

> ~ *Alfred North Whitehead, English mathematician and philosopher*

"You cannot do a kindness too soon because you never know how soon it will be too late."

> ~ *Ralph Waldo Emerson, American essayist, lecturer, philosopher, and poet*

"The deepest craving of human nature is the need to be appreciated."

> ~ *William James, American philosopher and psychologist*

"We can only be said to be alive in those moments when our hearts are conscious of our treasures."
> ~ *Thornton Wilder, American Playwright*

"Gratitude is the sign of noble souls."

> ~ *Aesop*

WISDOM

Women have important work to do, especially now and especially those of us who have lived more than a few decades. Women are stepping forward and daring to share what they have learned from their challenges and their deepest suffering in a way that is unprecedented.

One by one as we share our truth with courage, passion and compassion, we are not only changing the world, we are changing ourselves from the inside out. Each time we show up in the world authentically, our personal strength grows. Aligning our insides with our outsides makes us not only more resilient, but able to share the wisdom we have gained from our suffering.

Age honors women with deep intuition and wisdom. Our bodies may slow down and grow more fragile with each passing year; our minds may trip over memories and our tongues over words more often, but a deep, rich and wise river runs through us all. It is a potent source, a wellspring of wisdom and healing. We are emerging as shamans and prophets, teachers and guides to young and old alike.

As we turn away from our fascination with youth and accept the mantel of wisdom, we assume our proper place in the world. Our years of suffering, learning, successes and failures was our rite of passage. Now it is our responsibility to speak the truth, to share our wisdom and to show up as we are, wherever we are.

The world is in desperate need of the steady hand of wisdom, of truth, of integrity and intuition. A woman's wisdom -- refined by years of struggle, pain, and hardship, and her stubborn refusal to give in to despair, offers a perspective unavailable to the young. This perspective, achieved only in the living of life, reveals a more perfect understanding of the true nature of love, the need for forgiveness, and an unyielding willingness to continue on in hope. We possess a burgeoning inner knowledge that has no use for restrictions placed by worldly standards or external expectations.

The aging process inspires the development of our contemplative nature as well, if we allow it. This too is a gift, not only to the one who has made the shift, but to the world of the innocent that have yet to understand the depth of life and all that is.

We must not be afraid of what we have been given. It is our destiny. It is the world's necessity. It is its hunger. It is our hunger.

REFLECT on WISDOM

What does wisdom mean to you?

_____

_____

_____

_____

_____

_____

_____

_____

_____

_____

_____

How, when and where do you share your wisdom? Do you see any other options?

_____

_____

_____

_____

_____

_____

_____

_____

_____

_____

_____

_____

_____

_____

QUOTES ON WISDOM

"Keep me away from the wisdom which does not cry, the philosophy which does not laugh and the greatness which does not bow before children."
~Kahlil Gibran, Lebanese-American writer & poet,
Mirrors of the Soul

"Honesty is the first chapter in the book of wisdom."
~Thomas Jefferson,
3rd President of the United States,
"Letter to Nathaniel Bacon, 1813"

" Always choose the irrational wisdom of the heart over the cold analysis of the mind."
~Deepak Chopra, Indian-American author

"The soul always knows what to do to heal itself. The challenge is to silence the mind."
~Caroline Myss, American teacher & author

"Ours is not the task of fixing the entire world at once, but of stretching out to mend the part of the world that is within our reach."
~Dr. Clarissa Pinkola Estés,
American psychoanalyst & writer,
"Inspiration"

"Find your truth and live it in love, and your legacy will unfold bit by bit to find its place in the tapestry of eternity."
~Dorothy Sander, American writer
Founder of The Aging Abundantly Community

"Wisdom enables us to see beyond ego and to gain clarity where there might otherwise be confusion."
~Allan Lokos, American meditation teacher & author

"Even if you are a minority of one, the truth is the truth."
~Mahatma Gandhi, leader of India's
Independence Movement

"Old age is not a disease—it is strength and survivorship, triumph over all kinds of vicissitudes and disappointments, trials and illnesses."
~Maggie Kuhn,
American activist & founder of Gray Panthers,
in New Age magazine

"Wisdom grows in quiet places."
~Austin O'Malley, American professor & writer,
Keystones of Thought

"Those who dream by day are cognizant of many things which escape those who dream only by night."
~Edgar Allan Poe, American author & poet,
"Eleonora"

"Wisdom comes with the ability to be still. Just look and just listen. No more is needed. Being still, looking and listening activate the non-conceptual intelligence within you. Let stillness direct your words and actions."
~Eckhart Tolle,
Canadian author & spiritual teacher,
Stillness Speaks

"Your vision will become clear only when you can look into your own heart. Who looks outside, dreams; who looks inside, awakes."

~Carl Jung, Swiss psychiatrist & writer,
Memories, Dreams, Reflections

"If in fact the highest, most creative work is the work of consciousness, then in slowing down we're not doing less: we're doing more . . . Having slowed down physically we're in a better space to rev up psychically. We are becoming contemplative . . . We're going slower in order to go deeper, in order to go faster in the direction of urgently needed change in the world."

~Marianne Williamson, American author

"The best mind-altering drug is truth."

~Lily Tomlin, American comedian & author

ABUNDANCE

In the late 1990s while I was still in my 40s, homeschooling my children, and deeply involved in building and running our family business, a good friend of mine gave me a copy of Sarah Ban Breathnach's book Simple Abundance. I read bits and pieces of it on and off over the next couple of years. These essays inspired and challenged me to begin to change my life.

It wasn't until I crossed the threshold into my 50s and entered a decade of personal chaos and transformation that I picked Breathnach's book up again. This time I read it from cover to cover. It resonated with my deepest beliefs and values, some of which I'd set aside to pursue practical matters. Her words offered both a challenge to begin living a life more in tune with those beliefs and support from someone who understood the process.

As I read the essay of the day, I began to make changes, both in my perspective and lifestyle. I began to focus more on a life of inner abundance and less on a life of accomplishments and worldly abundance. This book led me back to myself and launched me into the transformative process.

When I began to think and write about life after 50, I could not think of a more appropriate concept than abundance to sum up the aging process. I did not, and still do not, believe that aging is only about suffering, loss, death, and gradual diminishment.

Instead, I see aging as a tremendous opportunity to bring decades of life experience to fruition. In countless ways, age creates a kind of abundance that youth simply cannot imagine. We must embrace that abundance.

As we age we become abundant in spirit, abundant in wisdom, and have an abundance of gifts to share with all who cross our path.

The last decades of our lives are packed with opportunity for transformation, personal and spiritual growth, and a freedom that defies the restrictions of the physical body and mind. Our spiritual nature is there to pick up the slack and as we embrace our own abundance, we free our spiritual energy to do its work. Gifts we never conceived or dreamed possible await our attention. They are right under our noses.

REFLECT on ABUDANCE

What does abundance mean to you?

_____

_____

_____

_____

_____

_____

_____

_____

_____

_____

What do you have more than enough of? What strengths and gifts have grown in recent years?

_____

_____

_____

_____

_____

_____

_____

_____

_____

_____

_____

_____

_____

QUOTES ON ABUNDANCE

"The hope for abundance can sometimes make people put up with all kinds of stuff that hurts their spirit. Self-love, trust, courage and the willingness to shake life up is sometimes needed in order to make and carry out whole being healthy choices."
~Sylvia Brallier, American artist & writer

"Doing what you love is the cornerstone of having abundance in your life."
~Dr. Wayne Dyer, American philosopher & author

"Abundance is not something we acquire. It is something we tune into."
~Dr. Wayne Dyer, American philosopher & author

"The test of our progress is not whether we add more to the abundance of those who have much, it is whether we provide enough for those who have little."
~Franklin D. Roosevelt,
32nd President of the United States,
"Presidential Inaugural Address," 1937

"The world breaks everyone, and afterward, some are strong at the broken places."
~Ernest Hemingway, American author,
A Farewell to Arms

"The butterfly counts not months but moments, and has time enough."
~Rabindranath Tagore, Bengali poet,
"I Touch God in My Song"

"Whatever we are waiting for—peace of mind, contentment, grace, the inner awareness of simple abundance—it will surely come to us, but only when we are ready to receive it with an open and grateful heart."

~Sarah Ban Breathnach, American author,
Simple Abundance

"The greatest good you can do for another is not just to share your riches but to reveal to him his own."

~Benjamin Disraeli (Earl of Beaconsfield),
British Prime Minister & writer

"Not what we have but what we enjoy, constitutes our abundance."

~Epicurus, philosopher of ancient Greece

"If you want to live peacefully, joyfully and abundantly in the years to come, you must walk your talk."

~Martha Beck, American sociologist & author,
"Cry Freedom!"

"I hope you will go out and let stories happen to you, and that you will work them, water them with your blood and tears and your laughter till they bloom, till you yourself burst into bloom."

~Dr. Clarissa Pinkola Estés,
American psychoanalyst & writer,
Women Who Run with the Wolves

"Once you deliberately focus on abundance, you'll be overwhelmed by all the good things that show up like manna in the desert, without much effort on your part."

~Martha Beck, American sociologist & author,
"Trust That You'll Find Exactly What You Need"

"As long as we remain vigilant at building our internal abundance—an abundance of integrity, an abundance of forgiveness, an abundance of service, an abundance of love—then external lack is bound to be temporary."

~Marianne Williamson, Everyday Grace: Having Hope,
Finding Forgiveness and Making Miracles

"Secret to having abundance: Stay focused on what you love and express it fearlessly."

~ Anonymous

"The fastest way to bring more wonderful examples of abundance into your personal experience is to take constant notice of the wonderful things that are already there."

~ Esther Hicks, American inspirational speaker
and author

"Remember, no more effort is required to aim high in life, to demand abundance and prosperity than is required to accept misery and poverty."

~ Napoleon Hill, American self-help author,
Think and Grow Rich

AFTERWORD

There are many great and inspiring teachings in the annals of our collective history. I hope you found comfort, joy and guidance in the small selection I shared here. These are among my favorites. I encourage you to look for and add your own.

Reading books that inspire us to think deeper thoughts and push us beyond the everyday are there to guide us through life. They inform the way in which we live. It's easy to become caught up in the mundane, everyday concerns that more readily catch our attention. Moving beyond the superficial and obvious requires a certain amount of intention and commitment. For me, it has been a worthwhile practice. I return to it again and again, especially during challenging times.

An daily practice of reflective reading is difficult to consistently maintain, but when we participate in this practice, we are strengthened and uplifted.

I encourage you to seek out teachers and writers that speak to the deeper parts of you. Take them on as your guides. In so doing you may wish to add your own quotes and teachings to this book. I have reserved several blank pages at the end of this volume just for that purpose.

If you enjoyed this book and found it valuable (and I hope that you did!), please share it with others who might benefit from a little inspiration. Like all independently published authors and writers, I hope my readers carry my message forward. I encourage and welcome your reviews on Amazon and Goodreads as well.

Please feel free to contact me via email: AgingAbundantly@gmail.com I love hearing from readers and value your input!

Dorothy Sander, 2018

ONLINE CONNECTIONS:

Website: AgingAbundantly.com
Facebook: www.facebook.com/pages/Aging-Abundantly
Twitter: @AgingAbundantly
Pinterest: http://www.pinterest.com/djsander/
Email: AgingAbundantly@gmail.com

Thank you!

"I hope you will go out and let stories happen to you, and that you will work them, water them with your blood and tears and your laughter till they bloom, 'till you yourself burst into bloom." ~Clarissa Pinkola Estes

FAVORITE QUOTES & REFLECTIONS

Made in the USA
Columbia, SC
10 March 2019

BATTLEGROUND

To my new family at Gold Hill with love and thanks

BATTLEGROUND

Lessons from the Life of Joshua

Stephen Gaukroger

Christian Focus

ISBN 1 85792 163 1

Published in 1997 by Christian Focus Publications,
Geanies House, Fearn, Ross-shire, IV20 1TW,
Great Britain.

Cover design by Donna Macleod

Printed in Great Britain by
The Guernsey Press Co Ltd,
Vale, Guernsey, Channel Islands.

Contents

Preface

This Bible teaching started its life in the study, made its first public appearance in the pulpit and now has arrived in print! (I am so grateful to all those – typists, editors and publishers – who made the journey from 'sermon to book' possible.)

The book you have in your hand follows the adventures of a remarkable leader. It attempts to describe the lessons of these adventures for both leaders and those who lead. Joshua was a military strategist, a political ruler, a skilled negotiator and, supremely, a spiritual leader. Everyone involved in leadership today can learn vital principles from this 'tough leader for tough times'. Whether you are leading a multinational company, a government department or struggling to lead a church or a cell-group – the character of Joshua and the book named after him has much to teach us.

And, of course, this book addresses questions of 'followership' as well as leadership. Good followers ultimately make excellent leaders! This book of Joshua highlights (sometimes with brutal honesty) what happens when a leader is let down by those he leads. It explores how failure can be resolved, and points to a model of community which involves both leader and led being submitted totally to God.

To some Christians, their knowledge of biblical principles starts with Matthew's gospel; the whole of the Old Testament is covered in a thick fog. What on earth can the tribal battles of a small, ancient people-group have to do with my life at the end of the twentieth century? I can only plead for Joshua to be given a chance to establish his relevance. For myself, I can say that as I have read these pages again I have been amazed to discover its value for my life, my work, my church – right now! The character of God, the dilemmas facing human beings, the principles of leadership .... all seem clearly unchanged.

Undoubtedly Joshua lived at a very different point in history and lived in a foreign culture to most of us. But once you have grappled with these differences valuable, permanently relevant principles confront us at every turn.

Stephen Gaukroger,
February, 1997.

Introduction

Anticipation plays a huge part in the Book of Joshua. The people of God, Israel, seem always to be on the verge of something, but then God appears to take them off at a tangent. This happens in all sorts of different ways. Joshua is a book of cliffhangers, a book where the reader is constantly wondering, 'What is going to happen next?'

The background

The story really begins with Abraham. God made great promises to him regarding his descendants, although he did inform Abraham that they would become slaves in Egypt before they would inherit the Promised Land (Genesis 15:13-16). The story moves on to Abraham's great-grandson, Joseph, sold by his brothers as a slave, but later, because of his ability to interpret dreams, he was made a great leader in Egypt. He also proved himself to be a man of great wisdom. One of his most notable achievements was a massive starvation-prevention programme to protect the Egyptians during a future seven-year famine which God had revealed in a dream of Pharaoh. When the famine arrived, Joseph's brothers came to Egypt to buy grain. They did not recognize Joseph to begin with. However, Joseph told them who he was, forgave them for selling him as a slave, and arranged for them and their families to stay in Egypt (Genesis 37-50).

Four hundred years passed by, until a Pharaoh arose who did not know of Joseph and who saw the Israelites as a threat to Egypt's security. Therefore he had them work as slaves.

God sent Moses and Aaron to deliver his people. The Pharaoh would not free the Israelites despite the nine plagues that God inflicted on the Egyptians. However, when all the firstborn of Egypt were killed in the tenth judgment, the people of God were at last set free (Exodus 1-11).

This momentous event was followed by Israel's journey through the desert to the Promised Land. It was a strange journey, with God showing his power and concern for them, and Israel revealing their obstinacy and rebelliousness towards God.

God had delivered the children of Israel from Egypt with a tremendous display of power, and followed this deliverance with another display of power, parting the Red Sea so that they could cross over on dry land. However, at Mount Sinai where he gave them his laws, the Israelites committed idolatry by worshipping a golden calf, for which many of them were punished by death (Exodus 12-20, 32).

When the Israelites reached the borders of Canaan, twelve spies were sent to survey the country. Although they all said the land was fertile, ten of the spies also said the inhabitants would be too powerful for the Israelites to conquer. Only Caleb and Joshua said that the Israelites could defeat them. But the Israelites refused to listen to Caleb and Joshua, and so were punished by God, who refused to let any who were over twenty years of age enter the Promised Land. Instead, the nation was to wait in the desert for thirty-eight years until those punished had all died. Caleb and Joshua, however, would enter the land (Numbers 13-14).

Joshua's personal history

Joshua was forty when the Israelites left Egypt. He was one of the two spies who came back saying, 'It's absolutely fantastic! Canaan is wonderful, let's go and inherit it. It's a fertile land, let's go and develop it. Never mind the giants, let's go and conquer it. It's what God has provided.'

At this point in his life, when he stood with Caleb, Joshua was preparing for leadership. But it was to be thirty-eight years before he was given an opportunity to lead the people. One aspect of his preparation was the strength he gained from standing firm when almost everybody else stood against him.

This is a reminder that many future leaders are prepared for greater things later on in their lives by the seemingly small decisions they make in the face of opposition. It is those who stand firm, whatever the cost, who are building characters that will stand them in good stead for significant ministry opportunities later.

Many people come into ministry late in life. It is a little known fact that many key people do not actually enter into their major life work until their sixties, and God gives them ten, fifteen, even twenty years of extraordinary ministry in the later part of their lives. Moses, for example, was eighty when he started coming into the fulness of his relationship with God. Joshua was forty when the Israelites left Egypt, forty-two when they stood on the verge of the Promised Land for the first time, and eighty years of age when at last he led the people of God into the Promised Land. He had become a man of wisdom, with many years of experience behind him.

Joshua went on to lead Israel for thirty years. In Joshua 24:29 we find that 'After these things, Joshua son of Nun, the servant of the LORD, died at the age of one hundred and ten.'

So the Book of Joshua is a chronicle of thirty years of a man of God's life.

In Joshua 1:1; 2:1 and 2:23 he is described as 'Joshua, the son of Nun.' When Moses sent out the twelve spies thirty-eight years earlier, two of them are described in this way – Joshua, the son of Nun, and Caleb, the son of Jephunneh. Why this stress on ancestry? Obviously the author believes it is important that we know who their ancestors were.

There are two possible reasons for this. One is that there may have been dozens of Joshuas and Calebs, and the writer is keen to make sure his readers know exactly which Joshua and Caleb he is referring to. But I suspect that is a minor reason, for their exploits were such that when one spoke about Joshua and Caleb, people knew exactly who was being referred to.

The second, more important reason is that the Old Testament writers gave relevance to the present by basing it on authority from the past. In other words they were saying, 'God did this and because he was reliable, we can be certain he will do it again in the future.' I suspect that Nun and Jephunneh were men whom God met. And it is as if the great Jewish faith is passed down. Joshua and Caleb were not just dropped into history, isolated from the past. The baton of faith had been passed from one generation to another, and Joshua and Caleb would pass it on through their families.

We too owe a great honour and debt to many people who, as it were, fathered and mothered us and brought us into the faith. We had Sunday School teachers, and pastors, and home group leaders, and others that we look back to. We praise God for them, because just like Paul 'fathered' Timothy, in the spiritual sense they 'fathered' us.

And we have a responsibility to pass the baton on to the next generation. In a relay race, the critical moment is when the baton is passed. The other stages in the race are less dangerous if the runners are gripping the baton tightly. It is really important that the message is passed from generation to generation, which is why work among the children and young people in a church is so important. God has no grandchildren, each generation must discover faith for itself, and then pass on the baton to others.

Supernatural history

I suspect that it was Joshua himself who wrote the events of these thirty years. He probably wrote about 1,400 years before Christ was born.

In the early years of this century, some liberal theologians tried to demystify the Bible by the process called demythologization. They tried to remove the supernatural elements from the Bible, in order to make it more acceptable to people. The Book of Joshua was one biblical book that suffered heavily in that revision, for they found it difficult to withdraw the supernatural from Joshua and end up with any book at all. The text is shot through with the supernatural; one cannot avoid seeing the fingerprints of God on each event described in the book.

An encounter with this book is not just an encounter with ancient history, though it is that. It is not just an encounter with a powerful, strategic planner and general, though it is that too (Joshua was described by General Patton, an American general, as probably the greatest strategist of the Old Testament). What we find in the Book of Joshua is God with his hand upon Joshua and upon his people, moving in miraculous power.

1

A new leader for a new era
Joshua 1:1-9

The children of Israel were poised on the edge of the Promised Land. Some commentators suggest they numbered about 2,000,000, but I think that is probably an over-statement. Certainly there were several hundred thousand men, women and children gathered by the ravine where the Jordan flows, looking across it to the flat land beyond; the Promised Land that was theirs for the taking.

Joshua, who had been given the tremendous responsibility of leading Israel, was in his eighties. I am sure he was somewhat apprehensive at the prospect of taking the place of Moses. Perhaps in his mind was a picture of Moses leading the people of God through forty years of wilderness wandering. Joshua had watched him year by year: 'How is this working out? What kind of man is this? How does he operate? How does he respond to stress and pressure? How does he respond to criticism of his leadership? How does he respond to advice from others?' Throughout these forty years of wandering Joshua was imbibing wisdom from his leader, Moses. Now the time had come for him to lead the people in to the Promised Land.

Preparing for a new era

> After the death of Moses the servant of the LORD, the LORD said
> to Joshua son of Nun, Moses' assistant: 'Moses my servant is
> dead. Now then, you and all these people, get ready to cross
> the Jordan River into the land I am about to give to them – to
> the Israelites. I will give you every place where you set your
> foot, as I promised Moses. Your territory will extend from the
> desert and from Lebanon to the great river, the Euphrates – all
> the Hittite country – and to the great sea on the west. No-one
> will be able to stand up against you all the days of your life. As
> I was with Moses, so I will be with you; I will never leave you
> or forsake you' (Joshua 1:1-5).

In verse 1, the name for God is LORD. The name so translated
is Yahweh. It was the sacred Jewish name for God meaning
'the Ever-living One'. So although Moses was dead, the Ever-
living One would go on being with Joshua.

The first phrase in verse 2, 'Moses, my servant is dead',
contains a profound message that we need to note: God is
telling Joshua, and through him the people of God, that the
era of Moses is finished. There is no point in looking back. A
new era is beginning, with Joshua at the head instead of
Moses.

We too, in the church today, need to take this message to
heart. There is always a tendency to look back whenever a
leader dies, or moves on. In church life it is very easy always
to want what happened yesterday. The stick-in-the-muds,
nose-in-a-ruts always want it to be yesterday, whereas the
trendy movers and shakers always want it to be tomorrow!
These are the dreadful diseases of the church. Where are the
people who want it to be *now*?

Perhaps God is saying to you to stop being held by the chains of yesterday, to stop looking back to what once was, to stop walking backwards into the future. Let go of the failures and the pains of yesterday. Offer them back to God, and do not let them grip your spirit any longer. Be released and freed from them. Then you will be aware of the presence of the Ever-living One.

God told Joshua to get ready

Here, right at the start of the Book of Joshua, we have the traffic lights of God's wisdom. To get ready is the amber light of preparation, before getting the green light to cross the Jordan into the Promised Land.

The Jordan was a national boundary. Crossing the Jordan would be a huge signal to the Canaanites that battle was about to commence. Crossing the Jordan was the point at which there would be no turning back.

Maybe you are standing at a crossing which involves a difficult decision, but you are aware that God is calling you to decide. It may be a decision to stay where you are, or it may be a decision to go on into something else. Maybe you

---

The Jordan river is actually very narrow, but what makes it so difficult to cross is that it is in a gorge. Most of the Jordan is below sea level. The sides of the gorge are crumbly and insecure, and as one gets near the edge of the Jordan, it is very easy to push the earth down into the river and even to fall into the gorge. Joshua 3 tells us that the river was in flood, therefore it was even more dangerous at that time. It was swelling up the banks of this gorge, which were insecure and very difficult to walk on.

are standing on that verge waiting for God to bless you, but he will only do so when you actually cross your Jordan. The God who is with you this side of the Jordan will also be with you on the other side. That is the nature of the God we serve and worship. He is always with us, even at the other side of difficult decisions.

God gave Joshua great promises

'Your territory will extend from the desert and from Lebanon to the great river, the Euphrates – all the Hittite country – and to the Great Sea on the west. No-one will be able to stand up against you all the days of your life' (verse 4). They were promises of conquering and victory.

True, the promises involved all of God's people, but God first gave the vision to Joshua as their leader. The promises were not a *carte blanche* for Joshua to assume that everything he did would turn to gold and that he would have no problems. But God was assuring him that the ultimate victory was his.

God also promised his presence to Joshua: 'As I was with Moses, so I will be with you' (verse 5). With God the best is always yet to be. He always has more things to enter into with those who lead his people. As God has been with past generations of Christian leaders, so he will be with leaders today as they face quite important decisions, and, every so often, crisis decisions that affect the course of the rest of their lives.

God encourages the new leader

'Be strong and courageous, because you will lead these people to inherit the land I swore to their forefathers to give them. Be strong and very courageous. Be careful to obey all the law my servant Moses gave you; do not turn from it to the right or to the left, that you may be successful wherever you go. Do not let this Book of the Law depart from your mouth; meditate on it day and night, so that you may be careful to do everything written in it. Then you will be prosperous and successful. Have I not commanded you? Be strong and courageous. Do not be terrified; do not be discouraged, for the LORD your God will be with you wherever you go' (Joshua 1:6-9).

After the death of Moses, Joshua's life took on new meaning. Following the example in life and death of this great man, Moses, Joshua put on the mantle of leadership. He was transformed from being number two, about whom very little was known, and thrust into the limelight to take the people of Israel on into the Promised Land. Joshua was a man with a mission, but a man struggling to come to terms with his calling by God. He was a man under pressure, a man fearful and afraid. And to that man, God said, 'Be strong and very courageous.'

Many leaders today need to hear this message of encouragement. There are many reasons why they can feel like Joshua did, facing the future with apprehension, unsure what it will bring. Perhaps they have been given roles and responsibilities they are not sure they can fulfil. They feel vulnerable, inadequate and insecure.

When God says, 'Be strong and very courageous,' it is almost rubbing salt in the wound, isn't it? There is nothing worse when you face a very difficult situation, than for another person to suggest the situation is easy. We can all face other people's problems with no great concern. But God said to Joshua, 'I am going to make you strong and very courageous.'

If we abuse our bodies by not resting properly or by eating too much of the wrong things, and not exercising at all, then inevitably our physical strength wanes and our overall level of fitness declines. There is a spiritual parallel with what God is saying to Joshua. God is not using throwaway words, he wants Joshua to play his part, he wants a commitment to the law, for Joshua to immerse himself in the Word. If Joshua plays his part in this, God will reward him with courage.

There is more than just an encouragement to do something however, there is a divine touch that can come into the lives of believers. God whispers in our ears, 'Be strong and courageous for I am going to be with you. I love you. You may be fearful right now but believe me, I will be with you.' When parents whisper a word of encouragement in their children's ears, it enables the children to do things they were too frightened to do on their own.

Joshua could be strong and courageous on the basis of three things: the promise of the land, the power of the Word, and the presence of the Lord. From these foundations we can extract three principles which still apply to leaders and to all believers today: God keeps his promise; God's Word is important; God will never forsake those who love him.

God keeps his promises

'Be strong and courageous, because you will lead these people to inherit the land I swore to their forefathers to give them' (verse 6).

When the Scripture says the land was promised to their forefathers, the phrase used is 'I swore it'. God commits himself by an oath, which is stronger than a promise. It is a guarantee of his commitment to this action. This is not a casual word by a friend that may or may not be fulfilled. The implication is this: God says, 'Remember Abraham, Isaac and Jacob? I declared that their descendants would be like the sand on the sea shore or the stars in the heavens. I swore that this land would be theirs and their descendants. That's why I took the Israelites out of the land of Egypt. So Joshua, be strong and very courageous.'

The critical thing is that God's Word can be trusted and relied upon. Sometimes I meet people who are searching to discover the truth of Christianity. They say, 'I want to be a Christian, but how can I be sure?' I tell them that every person has to come to God wanting forgiveness and cleansing. God has said he will turn nobody away, and his Word is absolutely certain. God always gives what he says he will give; his promises absolutely, unequivocally never fail.

But, it was no good Joshua sitting down on the side of Jordan saying, 'Well, God, you're going to be with me. That's really great! Wonderful!' Joshua would have to go over the Jordan. It is not until leaders and other Christians take action that the promise is tested. So many want a promise from God, but they want proof before they act, whereas God says to act on the promise.

God's Word is important

No-one is sure what the Word of God was at the time of Joshua. It may have been some of the Deuteronomic literature: the first five books of the Bible; it may have been some things related to the Ten Commandments and other documentation. But certainly it was a body of teaching of godly values.

The Israelites were to obey the Word, they were to keep the Word in their mouth, and they were to meditate on it day and night. Joshua needed to understand that if he was going to be strong and very courageous, he not only needed to stand on the promise of what God said he would do, but he needed to depend on the power of the Word that he had already been given. The law was there to guide him, to provide a moral framework within which he and the people of God could operate.

I can think of nothing that will give Christians more courage in the second half of the 1990s than the eternal Scripture. Obey the Word. Far too many Christians know the Bible, but do not obey it. There are many churches and leaders in this country who are sold out to the truth of Scripture. They love the Bible, they think it is very important, they know every single aspect of the book. They could tell you all the characters in the Book of Genesis. They know everything about the design of the Tabernacle. They know all about the visions in the Book of Revelation and what they mean. But is there obedience to the Word?

Never mind how much we know, do we *do* what the Word says? If we do not, then our knowledge of it is facile. It is no good saying that you know the Highway Code and then behaving like you do not. Obedience to the Bible is critical. Head knowledge is important, but we need to be obedient. We each have to say, 'My life must come under the authority of the Bible.'

If Joshua was not prepared to come under the authority of this Book of the Law, the people were under no obligation to follow him. But, because Joshua was under authority, they came under authority to him. That is any leader's claim to authority. If church leaders are submissive to the Word of God, then the membership should be submissive to their teaching of the Word. Leaders only have authority insofar as they are under submission to a higher authority – God in his Word.

When God told Joshua that the words were not to depart from his mouth, he was using a Hebrew phrase which means to 'eat the law'. Have you noticed that the more we talk about biblical things, the more we remember them, and the more we are excited by them? If we are passionately interested in a hobby we will speak about its obscure details enthusiastically. I am like that about books. I can tell you about authors and the number of books they have written. I know which publishers relate to what theological positions. I talk about it all the time with anybody who will listen – and very few will! I can't help it! It's what drives me, it's what impassions me, it's what motivates part of my life. It is what is in my mouth.

These words to Joshua are an instruction to keep fresh his love of Scripture. Leaders today too are to talk about the Scripture, its principles and values; to speak about its characters; to mention the Lord and all he has done. The more they talk about it, the more they will encourage other Christians to grow and to learn and to share together. All these things generate a knowledge and a love for the Word. Sadly, Christian leaders today can be so dominated by trivia that they do not always have time for the things of Scripture. Some are so busy that they do not have the time to meditate. They read the Bible, but the meditative task – the ruminating, the thinking, the prayer – evades them.

Joshua was an army captain, a kind of prophet, a political leader. He had a lot of people to lead, but in all the busyness of his responsibilities, he had to have time to reflect on the law of God. If he did not, in the activity of conquest he would be drawing on a reduced supply of inner strength.

This is an important word to the hectic activity of the late twentieth century. In their busyness leaders can be so dominated by the urgent, that they totally miss the important. *The important ought to outweigh the urgent.*

God will be with you

'For the LORD your God will be with you wherever you go' (verse 9). The Lord is with leaders, as with all believers, as the presence of the Spirit lives within them. Leaders need his presence day by day, because sometimes they feel very alone, as Joshua must have felt from time to time as he realized his responsibility to lead these thousands of people.

These words from verse 9 are worth reminding ourselves of daily. For many leaders there will be times when they feel broken, despairing and totally finished – but God will be there. He is with us in the very good and in the very bad, and in everything in between. He loves us and is never going to leave us.

2

The people to lead
Joshua 1:10-17

Joshua ordered the officers (a Hebrew word referring to those who kept the register of the people), 'Go through the camp and tell the people, "Get your supplies ready. Three days from now you will cross the Jordan here to go in and take possession of the land the LORD your God is giving you for our own"' (1:10-11).

Supplies here is a deliberate choice of word. All through their years in the desert God gave them manna every day. Yet on the verge of the Promised Land, God suddenly said, 'Get supplies together.' The daily supply of manna was ending, and the people were now being encouraged to glean from the land around them, in which some of them were going to dwell permanently.

To do so, they had to follow Joshua and the other leaders of Israel. But what does 'following' mean? I can see at least five aspects in this section of the Book of Joshua.

1. Leading a people of faith
D-Day, the decisive day when the wilderness wandering was to be over for ever was near. The Promised Land must be taken. The Israelites had a promise from God that he would give them the land. But they would come into its possession as they stepped out and actually took the land.

Notice the present continuous tense in the statement

25

concerning God's promise. Joshua does not say, 'God *has given* you the land', although there is a sense in which that is true. Instead he says, 'Take possession of the land the LORD your God *is giving* you for your own.' Joshua's emphasis is a very helpful one for us to remember. He is not saying, 'God has given the land to you, therefore just wander into it and it will all be yours.' No, Joshua is saying, 'As you go and possess the land, God will progressively give it to you.' In other words, the promise of God is received by the activity of faith.

'Three days from now, you will cross the Jordan here ...' By virtue of their geographical location the Israelites were clustered together, almost forced into a kind of funnel arrangement, ready to go pulsating across the Jordan, and into the Promised Land. The River Jabbok kept them from moving south and the mountains kept them from heading north. Therefore they were not spread out along a lengthy front, but they were carefully targeted, ready in tight formation, to burst into the Promised Land.

Throughout the Scriptures there is a tremendous emphasis on this dual nature of accomplishing things: the authority and promise of God on the one hand, and human obedience on the other. This is a huge mystery, which we will have to grapple with. Is God sovereign and powerful, and able to carry out his purposes without any human help? Yes, he is not at all dependent on his people. And yet, he chooses, in an incredible way, to self-limit himself in order that his promises can be received by faith.

Hebrews 11 details incidents involving some who entered into the promises of God by faith. By faith Noah built a boat to save his family and the animal species, when he probably was not sure what the promise of rain meant. By faith Abraham realized that his descendants would be like the sand

on the seashore or the stars in the heavens in number. By faith
Gideon defeated the Midianites.

The only way these promises were realized was by the
people of God exercising faith in the promise. And the only
way the Promised Land was subdued was because the people
exercised faith in the promise of God.

Christians have to understand what it means to take a step
of faith which includes thinking, working and praying, and
sometimes being cautious. Caution, however, can also be
ungodly. Believers need to discern the difference, to ensure
we are not acting out of complacency or presumption, but are
acting out of faith. As we as churches or individuals consider
what is ahead, we will not possess the land if we stand back
and wait until every single thing is in place. There are steps
of faith that we need to take.

2. Fighting together

Joshua had a different message for the Reubenites, the Gadites
and the half-tribe of Manasseh. To them he said, 'Remember
the command that Moses, the servant of the LORD, gave you:
"The LORD your God is giving you rest, and has granted you
this land. Your wives, your children and your livestock may
stay in the land that Moses gave you east of the Jordan, but
all your fighting men, fully armed, must cross ahead of your
brothers. You are to help your brothers until the LORD gives
them rest"' (1:12-13).

Joshua realized that the three tribes could not be at rest
until all their brothers were at rest as well. He knew too that
their fighting men were needed to help conquer the land west
of the Jordan. It is absolutely thrilling the way these tribes
agree to obey Joshua just as they had obeyed Moses before

him. I consider this to be one of the greatest Old Testament examples of selflessness, for perhaps some of those fighting men of Reuben, Gad and Manasseh died in the invasion of Canaan. They gave their lives not for their own immediate kith and kin, but for the broader good of the people of God.

I find this sacrifice immensely challenging. Sometimes we will make sacrifices for members of our human family. We will do things for our children, or for our partner, or for our parents, and that is right. But when we became Christians we joined a bigger family, and God's calling for his people is for them to be characterized as those who pour out their lives for the broader family, and not just for those about whom they feel immediate concern.

This real challenge will mark out the difference between those who are Christian in name, and those whose lives count for God and who are prepared to lay down their lives for those who are not part of their immediate family. Our brothers and sisters exist in every corner of the world, and we are called to love them and have concern for them all.

3. Possessors of God's rest

The word 'rest' used in verse 13 is a technical word which has both a personal and a corporate application. In the corporate sense, it means to settle down. In the ancient world,

The Reubenites, the Gadites and the half-tribe of Manasseh were descendants of the sons of Jacob. Manasseh was one of Joseph's sons, the other was Ephraim. Joseph's sons' descendants were each regarded as a separate tribe. These three groupings were given special treatment in the sense that their territory was to be on the east of the Jordan rather than over on the other side.

it meant not just pitching your tent, but building a building, settling down in a community. The Israelites had been tented for forty years. They had never slept in the same pitch for more than a few weeks at a time. They were always moving on. Now Joshua says to these people, 'You have found your rest. You as a people have found a place to settle and you have found a place you can call home.'

In the personal sense, it means the rest which comes after exertion, after pressure. It means the rest that comes after a series of energetic tasks when one sits down and tries to recover. It is almost the feeling of coming home after a very long day at work. Personal rest is entering into a period when our exertions are finished and we just take a deep breath and relax.

But Joshua knows that these three tribes could not really rest in that fullest sense until their brothers had also found rest. Some Christians have come into God's rest. But genuine, biblical faith demands that as long as there are those believers who are not at rest, then those who are have a responsibility to be exercising love, time and energy on their behalf. How we need God's compassion to look around and not judge on the external outward appearance! Will we be those who, out of our rest, bring peace and rest to others who are rest-less?

4. Willing, obedient followers of God

The people then answered Joshua, 'Whatever you have commanded us, we will do, and wherever you send us, we will go' (1:16). No wonder Joshua did such mighty exploits. He was followed by a people who were committed not to him primarily, but to his God. Their prayer was, 'Only may the LORD your God be with you as he was with Moses' (verse

17). They saw Joshua as the human representation of the divine authority.

Sometimes people say to me, 'Steve, we want you to know we are right behind you.' What I want to know is, how far behind? Leaders, even when doing something that they believe is right, occasionally look over their shoulders to see if anybody is following.

The tribes of Reuben, Gad and Manasseh were more than only willing to help their fellow Israelites. Joshua asked them to go over ahead of their brothers. In other words, they were not a good distance behind Joshua, they were right up at the front with him, taking the flak in the hottest part of the battle.

In ancient battles, commanders knew exactly where the heat was going to be and there they put their best soldiers. The initial confrontation would take place between the crack troops. And so it was for these three tribes going ahead of all the rest of the troops. They were prepared to be the shock troops. They were prepared to be right in the dangerous place with their leader.

We need soldiers like those of Reuben and Gad and Manasseh in all our churches in this nation. We need people who will say, 'Yes, God has blessed us in many ways. But we're not sitting on our laurels, we are going to be right there at the front, telling others about the Lord, giving, praying, working, moving towards establishing the kingdom of God wherever we happen to find ourselves.'

How we need people in churches in this nation to be committed primarily to God and consequently to their leaders! And I say that without apology. The whole biblical thrust about people who are willing to follow, in a godly and committed way, needs re-emphasizing again and again.

Without obedient, committed followers, no leadership can be effective.

5. Encouraging their leader

The Moses generation died in the wilderness, and Moses' style of leadership became inappropriate for the conquering of the land. Moses' and Joshua's leadership styles were very different, but each was appropriate for the time. The tribes of Reuben, Gad and Manasseh did not pray that God would make Joshua the same as Moses. Rather, they prayed that God would be with Joshua as he had been with Moses, and if he was, they would follow Joshua. They were really following God.

God does not change. That is why there should not be a generation gap in the church. My grandfather preached the gospel in the West Riding of Yorkshire faithfully and regularly over many years. He and I had all sorts of arguments and discussions about what was appropriate in terms of presenting the gospel. We often disagreed about the way the Christian faith ought to be communicated. Yet he preached the gospel, and men and women found faith through his preaching. I pray that God will enable me to preach the gospel and that people will find faith through my preaching, even though the packaging is different, because it is a different generation that I am ministering to.

I remember speaking at a meeting in which the chairman was 80, the pianist was 89, the offering was taken by a lady who was 91. You can tell I was at a youth meeting! It was a very interesting meeting. I met a number of people in that age group whose faith shone so clearly that it was almost touchable. They were from a different era, but they loved Jesus.

It is easy for us to be dismissive or critical of people of another generation. When you next go to church, look around the congregation. There are the older characters and there are the new, emerging people. The style of dress, or the culture which surrounds it, or all the trappings, are not important. What is important is the God who stays the same.

The Israelites knew that the God who had kept them safe through years of wilderness wandering, was the same God who was now going to take them into the Promised Land, albeit with a new style of leadership and a new approach to the same God.

Most churches today are standing metaphorically on the verge of a Jordan, to some extent. How to proceed? The old structures may not work. The old things that helped to make decisions may not help us, but God is still the same. He never changes. He really is the same yesterday, today and for ever.

Having said that, I do not think church members today would be advised to say to their leaders what these tribes went on to say to Joshua: 'Whoever rebels against your word and does not obey your words, whatever you may command them, will be put to death.' That is on the strong side for twentieth century notions. But perhaps it would be useful from time to time as a threat!

What the tribes were saying, however, was that they were serious about their commitment to following Joshua. It was not just words. The tribes said, 'Only be strong and courageous.' They were great cheerleaders. 'Joshua, go for it! All power to you! Don't hold back! Don't be bullied by what you might find over there! Yes, there might be huge giants in the land. Yes, the river Jordan might be deep and difficult to cross. But go for it! Be strong and very courageous.'

Many church leaders have known the devastating disappointment of having been promised too much by others. Taking a huge risk and stepping out in faith, they then look behind and those who promised to be with them are not there. I meet those disappointed leaders from time to time. But these three tribes meant it, and it was tremendous for Joshua.

When Martin Luther King was preaching his heart out on the steps of the Capitol Building in Washington, how did he preach so well? Yes, he was a brilliant communicator, but there was a man beside him, shouting in his ear every few minutes, 'Preach it, Martin! Preach it!'

Joshua learned that these tribes would be with him. They were going to stand alongside him, no matter what happened. They cared for Joshua and for the people of God.

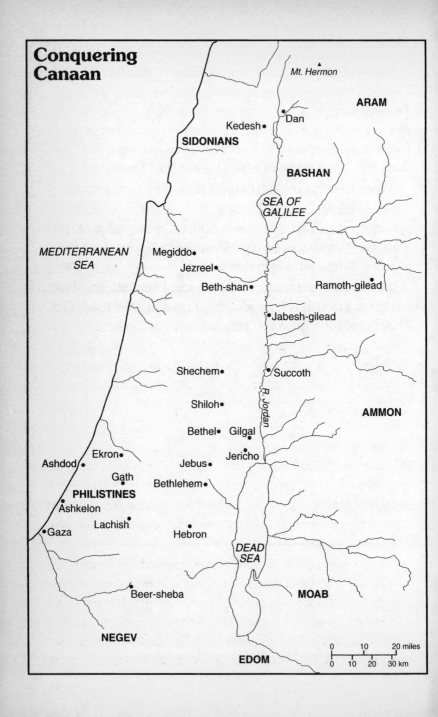

Conquering Canaan

Mt. Hermon

ARAM

Kedesh•   •Dan

SIDONIANS

BASHAN

SEA OF GALILEE

MEDITERRANEAN SEA

Megiddo•

Jezreel•

Beth-shan•   Ramoth-gilead•

•Jabesh-gilead

Shechem•   •Succoth

Shiloh•   **AMMON**

Bethel• •Gilgal

Ekron•   •Jericho

Ashdod•   Jebus•

Gath•   Bethlehem•

PHILISTINES

•Ashkelon

•Gaza   Lachish•

Hebron•   *DEAD SEA*

•Beer-sheba   **MOAB**

NEGEV

EDOM

0		10		20 miles
0	10	20	30 km	

3

An unlikely follower
Joshua 2:1-11

In Joshua chapters 2 to 4 there is described a period of supernatural experiences in the lives of the people of God. Many of these stories defy human imagination. They offend our minds. We read them and we think, How on earth could that have been? There is incident after incident in which God interjected himself in an incredible way into the affairs of ordinary men and women. In the Book of Joshua truth is stranger than fiction. And though it appears in places to be incredible, it has the stamp of truth and the mark of history upon it.

Spying out Jericho
At the start of chapter 2 we read that Joshua told two spies to go and look over the land, especially Jericho. Joshua was a military strategist and he knew that unless Jericho was conquered, nothing would succeed in the land of Canaan. Jericho was a key city.

So the spies went to Jericho and entered the house of a prostitute named Rahab and stayed there. Some commentators suggest that Rahab was actually an inn-keeper. Possibly they are embarrassed about the idea of prostitution and think it unlikely that God would have any dealings with someone who had sunk so low. I think it more likely that the spies'

Jericho was one of the few major cities that was hundreds of feet below sea level (it still is today). It was in a valley and guarded a pass. Towering each side, to the west and east, are huge mountain ranges. Therefore the way to get through and into possessing the whole of the land, was through this valley in the centre of which stood the city of Jericho. Joshua was determined that Jericho was the first target. If it was not destroyed, the children of Israel could not go into the Promised Land.

presence in the city had aroused suspicion and they were being chased by some of Jericho's security men. I reckon that in the panic of the chase they found their way into Rahab's house by accident.

Certainly there is nothing in the story to indicate that they went to the prostitute's house for the sake of the immoral activity for which she was known. This was not something they were doing while they were reconnoitring the city. They went to her house for safety.

Rahab's occupation gives us a glimpse of the kind of place the Israelites were moving in to. Prostitution was plied freely in the whole Jericho valley area; an area known for easy access to men and women who would provide sexual favours for the traveller in that part of Canaan. There were no established moral laws such as those of the Israelites, and so licentiousness was common. Jericho was not a 'nice' town, nor were its people upright.

Yet God took this sinful woman and turned her into a rescue package for the people of God. She is mentioned in Matthew 1 as being in the line from Abraham through David to Jesus. We have to recognize that Rahab the prostitute is a great symbol of the way God takes, and changes into powerful forces for good, people who are regarded by society as beyond the pale. It is a reminder that God is far more loving and all-inclusive and accepting than the church has sometimes been.

Rahab also shows that no-one is ever beyond being able to be used by God, if he or she has got a right spirit and attitude to him and his people. However low a person has sunk, however sinful some may feel they are, and however much a failure others may feel they are, there never comes a point where they are beyond God's ability to use them to touch and bless his people.

I find the story of Rahab tremendously reassuring, because the church in our country has traditionally been much more successful among those who would describe themselves as 'nice' and 'pleasant'. Certainly, the middle classes in our country have often been those places in which the church has flourished and grown; but among the aristocracy on one hand, and the working class on the other, the church has rarely flourished in this land.

And I think that is partly because of the attitudes of the people of God. Sometimes we are 'nicer' than God himself, and we need to be delivered from that attitude, so that we recognize his care and compassion and love for the hurting and the needy and the broken. We need to look at those caught in sin of whatever kind, through the eyes of Christ and not through the judgmental eyes of some kind of middle class society that looks down on others. That attitude has no place in the Body of Christ.

Many Christians need an attitude change. They are too quick to distance themselves from people who are of a different colour, or from a different background, or who dress in a different style, or who have sinned in a particular way. But the attitude of Scripture does not reflect many of the middle class values of the late twentieth century church in Britain.

Rahab's deception

In Joshua 2:1-7 we read how the spies entered Rahab's house and hid there. The king of Jericho was told, and sent the message to Rahab: 'Bring out the men who came to you and entered your house, because they have come to spy out the whole land.' Rahab answered rather coyly, 'Yes, the men did come to me, but I did not know where they had come from.' In other words, 'Lots of men come into this house. That is the nature of the house. Which two men are you thinking of?'

Rahab knew exactly which men they were looking for but deliberately lies to cover their tracks: 'At dusk, when it was time to close the city gate, the men left. I don't know which way they went. Go after them quickly. You may catch up with them.' And all the while the spies were hiding under stalks of flax laid out on the roof.

Rahab's deception raises a very difficult theological question. Was Rahab right to tell a lie to save the lives of the two spies? Or should she have said, 'Oh yes, of course, I know the two men of whom you speak. Come in, take them away, they are spies.' Would she have been right to say that, or should she have been evasive rather than lie directly, as certain commentators on this text have suggested?

The debate that has been in the church for many years is this: Is there some higher good that ought to be appealed to here? Was it appropriate for her to lie, because two people's lives were at stake? Or take another example: someone bursts into a house and asks the husband if his wife is there, with the intent of raping her. Would it be right to lie in this particular case?

Let me just say this about the Scriptures; they make no comment at this point about whether God approves of Rahab's lie or not. The text simply states what happened. It is a very difficult question, and one that the Bible does not address in this context.

And anyway, the woman was a prostitute, so worrying about whether or not she was right to lie is missing the point. The whole thrust is that these are real people, doing real things that come naturally and easily to them.

Real people handle real issues and sometimes get it wrong. And yet God uses their action. Amazing! This is the point of the passage; sometimes we make wrong decisions. This week we may have decided to do something that has caused pain, grief, disappointment and frustration to ourselves and others. We may have spoken in a way which has caused pain for ourselves and others.

All that may happen, but it is not the end. When the heart is repentant God can take all of the wrong and can turn it round and put it right. We do not live perfect lives from Sunday to Sunday. We do not get it right constantly day by day. We react emotionally; we react negatively; we react quickly and without thought. We speak when we ought to remain silent. We remain silent when we ought to speak. We act in haste, we act in anger, we act in frustration, we act out of resentment, we act out of jealousy, we act out of greed. So many of our actions are wrong, even though Christ is at work in our lives.

And yet God still comes by his glorious Spirit. This is the miracle of Christian faith. In all our sin, he comes like he came to a lying prostitute, and took what she did and brought blessing out of it. And so, whatever kind of day we have had, he comes to us, and as we reach to him and say, 'God, I have messed up this day,' he will take us right where we are. That is one of the things that thrills me most about this story.

Rahab's faith

The spies hiding under the flax on Rahab's roof had been sent to Jericho by Joshua to gather intelligence of two kinds. First, there was the military information regarding the battlements; how well the town was fortified, when the guards changed, the location of any vulnerable places, and so on. Secondly, Joshua wanted to know about the morale of the people in Jericho; were they ready for a fight, or were they terrified? The morale of an army is almost more important than the weaponry at its disposal.

That is as true today as it was then, despite the sophistication of modern weaponry. If the Gulf War taught anything, it taught that the destruction of a nation's morale is as important as overwhelming it in terms of military might.

Rahab volunteered a wonderful piece of information: 'I know the LORD has given this land to you, and a great fear of you has fallen on us, so that all who live in this country are melting in fear because of you.' The inhabitants were terrified of the Israelites, they were melting in fear into nothingness. Why was this? Not because Joshua's military might was known. Even Rahab the prostitute recognized that it was not massive military might that terrified her people, but the recognition that the Lord had given his people the victory.

At some point in the previous forty years, the news would have reached Jericho about a sea which had been dried up, because this group were so incredibly in touch with the God of the ages that he had made a path through the sea for them to escape a pursuing enemy. This was a God the like of which the Canaanites had never come into contact with before. This was a God to be afraid of. The people of Jericho also knew what had happened to Sihon and Og, the two kings of the Amorites east of the Jordan. It was not too long ago for this event to have been lost from memory.

'When we heard of it, our hearts sank and everyone's courage failed because of you, for the LORD your God is God in heaven above and on the earth below.' Rahab recognized that power is not located in military might or numerical strength, but in the God who is the God of heaven above and earth below. Not only is he God of the ages, not only is he God of the entire planet, but he is a God with heavenly authority over all the spirit beings and he is God over all the powers of the earth. Rahab knew that and was rightly afraid, and she realized that God had given Jericho into Israel's hands.

Faith for today

Rahab had realized that all the other gods she knew about were nothing in comparison with the great God of the Universe. This challenges me about how Christians find themselves in a world of petty gods and deities. They are no longer called Baal or Ashtaroth, but they have all sorts of other names; names related to other world religions, cults, or sects. They have names related to ideologies and ideas like materialism.

All these are present in our world, and can cause us to fear; who will succeed, who will win, what is it that will actually conquer the hearts and minds of the people of our planet, what philosophy will shape the world and change the way we live within it?

Until ten or fifteen years ago, many Christians lived in constant fear of the communist world. Its stated aim was to bring communism to nation after nation, and tear down democratic governments and bring about the domination of Marxist-Leninist philosophy, or at least something loosely linked to it. And many free democratic nations and many Christians lived in fear of that prospect. And then the Berlin Wall came down, and *glasnost* and *perestroika* changed the shape of our planet. Communism, far from being the course that dominated the world, ended up being a broken and defeated ideology in many parts of the world. It left God out, and ultimately God left it out of his plans.

And yet we still feel that something else will win the hearts and minds of the people of the world. We fear so much of what we see on our television screens or in our newspapers. We fear the onward march of Islam and other false religions.

Our response to all these things will depend largely on how secure we are in godly worship. Our God will not be put off by wars and rumours of wars. He is not taken by surprise by new developments in various nations. A think-tank here and a think-tank there will not come up with a fresh idea that confuses God, or catches him off his guard.

We live in a world where insecurity is written into the very fabric of existence, because of the rapid pace of change. Many of us barely manage to stave off the fear that we will not cope with all the changes. Or if we cope with it now, will we still cope with it when we are older?

Many of the very elderly people I am in contact with struggle to come to terms with a world that has changed beyond all recognition to the one they grew up in. They feel frightened; they feel alone; they feel it is not their world any more. It is cascading out of control. How can they know security and strength? So much causes them to be insecure.

And if people in middle-age are honest as they look at the rapidly developing world, some of them are frightened too. What will it mean? How secure is my job? How secure is my company? How secure is the future of our country? What will it mean for the Christian church? What will it mean for me as an individual?

Fear comes so easily. It can be trivial; If computers take over the world, where will that leave me as I am not computer-literate? Or it can be something that threatens our very livelihood, threatens our point of security, because the world has become such a different place. Perhaps the street in which you live was once filled with familiar faces. But now they have all moved away, and you dare not leave the house after dark. You are afraid of the knock on the door, and the loud riotous noises well after midnight that make it difficult for you to sleep.

How much we need Rahab's insight, that we, as the people of God, have a God who is all-powerful and who will never be obsolete. This is one of the most wonderful privileges of the Christian faith.

Many things we buy have built-in obsolescence. They are designed to wear out in a fairly short space of time. Otherwise you would not need a new one. We live in a throwaway society, where trends and fashion come and go.

In the face of the planned obsolescence of the twentieth century, we can have confidence in a God who never changes. We have a God who will not be taken by surprise, no matter what the future may bring. We have a God who can cope with whatever may come into my life and yours.

He is a God who rules the heavens and the earth. We can be secure in the knowledge that we worship a God who is never caught off guard and who never fails. No development on the global scene, no development on the individual scene will ever catch him out. Nothing that happens will ever cause God to shudder.

The two spies escape

When the immediate danger was past Rahab let the spies down by a rope through the window, for the house she lived in was part of the city wall. She instructed them, 'Go to the hills for the pursuers will not find you. Hide yourselves there three days until they return and then go on your way.' The hills Rahab was referring to were about half a mile to the east of the city. They were limestone rocks, about 1,500 feet high, and chiselled into them were all sorts of rock faces which became caves. Some of them had been hollowed out by small animals; others by brigands who used them as a base from which to come down into the plain and maraud anybody coming into or out of Jericho. Rahab sent the spies to a well-known local maze, where it would be very difficult to find them.

Before they left, Rahab had made the spies swear that they would preserve her life when they seized Jericho. The men said to her, 'This oath you made us swear will not be binding on us unless, when we enter the land, you have tied this scarlet cord in the window through which you let us down.' Scarlet is often seen in the Old Testament as being associated with sinfulness. There is some evidence to suggest that a prostitute would wear a scarlet colour. The cord could be a sign of where a prostitute is, but it was the sign of grace for Rahab.

A change of outlook

Incredible changes had occurred in Rahab's life. As a prostitute it is possible she would have had no dealings with men at all, apart from for sexual purposes. So actually to speak to them, let alone offer them shelter, was unusual. Also Rahab was a Canaanite, yet she put herself at risk to help the two Israelite spies. It is thrilling that God performed such a work of grace in breaking down the formidable obstacle of different nationalities. How we need the God of Rahab in our church and in our nation and in our world, to break down the prejudices between individuals and let people relate, not on the basis of colour or nationality, but on the basis of a relationship with God.

This passage points beyond Rahab the Canaanite and beyond the two Israelite spies to the God who can change men and women's hearts so that the bitter prejudices and deep divides that grip them can be removed by an encounter with him.

Not only was prejudice broken down, but Rahab appealed to be dealt with kindness. The word used here is the same word that is used about 250 times in the Hebrew Old Testament. It is a word which means God's covenant love to his people. It is usually used of God to an individual, rather than one individual to another individual.

God says to a person, 'I will love you although you don't deserve it. I have made a commitment to love you and I am going to go on loving you, whatever you have done or said,

and whatever you will go on to do or say. I am committed to
you and I am going to treat you kindly, even though you don't
deserve anything but justice.'

Sadly there are those whose prejudices in their relationship
with other human beings have been only partially broken
down, leaving an uneasy peace, and the 'We wouldn't be
critical in public' kind of statement. But the Bible calls us to
be kind to our enemies as well as to our friends.

Some Christians have made very important steps in
relationships in the church, but have not reached the step of
forgiving one another. They are still at the baby stage of
Christian understanding. They think justice is the important
thing.

Then there is the more mature stage, which is: 'I forgive
you. Jesus forgave me, I must forgive you. The Lord's prayer
says unless I forgive you, I can't be forgiven myself.' Some
operate along that level.

But to be treated with kindness is the next stage. It is
relatively easy for me to say, 'I forgive you for all you have
done.' But it is much harder to say, 'Not only do I forgive
you, but I will demonstrate that by treating you kindly.' That
is the ultimate step, and how difficult it is.

May God make us kind people as well as people who are
forgiving and who have had our prejudices and mis-
conceptions dealt with by him.

Kept safe

In response to the spies' suggestion, Rahab put the scarlet
cord in her window. Later, when the Israelites marched round
the city for several days, every time they walked round they
would see the cord in the window of Rahab's house. The

symbolism is interesting, not simply because scarlet represented sin and yet God was using it as a sign of grace, but also it was reminiscent of the sign on the doorposts many years earlier, when the children of Israel were about to come out of Egypt. In order for them to be protected from the angel of death who hovered over the land of Egypt, God instructed the Israelites to put blood on the lintel and the doorpost of their houses.

Rahab was about to avoid physical death. But not only this; she went on from this situation, set free to be the woman she had the potential to be. The superstructure of the city was destroyed eventually, but she and her family were kept safe. She was set free from a structure which made her depend on prostitution for her livelihood, and she came into a new set of relationships with God's covenant people.

Of course, her concern did not stop at herself, but included all her family. What an incredible picture of the evangelistic zeal that God wants for his people today! And the spies agreed to her request for her relatives to be protected, provided they were all in her house when the city was attacked.

The spies took Rahab's advice and headed for the caves where they hid for three days. Although the men from Jericho searched for the spies, they were not to be found. When the

---

It seems likely from what we know of Jericho at this period, that there was an overcrowding problem, so they had built houses on the city wall. Probably the second-rate accommodation was in the wall. It obviously was the most dangerous place to be, because it was the place that took the first brunt of an attack. Rahab's house would have been quite sizeable, almost like a cave, because she could get the rest of her family into it.

spies returned to Joshua with the report, what excitement there must have been!

So the children of Israel were poised to make a major step forward in their history. The conquering of the very first part of Canaan, the land immediately to the east of Jericho, and then Jericho itself. They could go with confidence because the Lord had given them the land. But also with the help of an ordinary individual called Rahab. In a sense, a whole nation had its future decided by one lowly woman.

4

Freeing the people from their past
Joshua 3:1-6

The children of Israel on the east of Jordan, while impatient
to get across and find a permanent place to live, had probably
become bemused while they waited for their leaders to decide
what to do. But now, the confusion was over.

Moving on, not back
Early in the morning, Joshua and all the Israelites set out
from Shittim (3:1). Shittim was known for acacia trees, it
was a beautiful spot and well-watered. It had groves of trees
and bushes, not at all like the desert. A beautiful place to be.
But guess what? They had been there before!

Years earlier, when Moses was their leader, the Israelites
had been led by the Moabites into sexual immorality and into
the worship of various Baals in that place of acacia bushes.
Shittim became synonymous with diseased religion. Although
the Israelites now under Joshua would only have been children
then, there was still a reminder of what had gone wrong years
before. But this time they were not moving backwards into
sin, but onwards towards the Jordan and to victory.

Like the Israelites, many Christians discover themselves
to be once again in situations that they were in before. The
sinful mess you may find yourself in now, is the one you were
in last year or ten years ago. You thought you would never get
to this point again, but you are back. You do have a choice,

however, either to go on to victory and conquest or to go
back into the wilderness for another bout of failure and sin.

God wants to move all his people on into victory and not
back into sinfulness. But how easy it is to hover where we
are, in our failure, in our sinfulness, when God has a glorious
future for us. His goal for every Christian is that we become
like Christ.

On a war-footing

The Israelites went to the Jordan where they camped before
crossing over (3:2). They had left the plain where Shittim
was located, and had come down on to another plain near to
the Jordan. The people of God moved out from the comfort
and the beautiful scenery, out from the shade and into the hot
desert, to a place where there were few provisions. But they
were ready for the battle.

As Christians, we too are to live on a wartime footing.
We are engaged in warfare against Satan, against all the
powers of darkness, against the evil that works itself out in
sinful men and women or in evil social structures or the
temptations that come to our own hearts through the luring of
the evil one. Christians are in a war situation not in a
playground (which is where many Christians seem to think
they are).

As Christians we ought to be living our lives in a way that
is different from non-Christians. We are gearing for battle.
We ought to be ready, stripped down for active service, making
sure that our time is not wasted. Of course, we need some
rest; even in wartime there is time for regrouping, rest and
recovery.

But we are engaged in warfare and we must be careful not

to become weighed down with all sorts of things, legitimate in themselves, but which actually lock us into this world in a way that God does not want.

When I was growing up, the great sin of the time was television. Anybody who had a television was flirting with Satan. After a while we got a television. The first programme I ever watched was a gardening programme. And I sat there trying to see how this could be sinful. It was just absurd. We can get so blocked in to irrelevant nonsense regarding worldliness, that we do not focus on what God is actually saying to us. If our television sets master us, we are in the wrong. But that is not to say it is wrong to own a television. It is our attitude to it that is wrong.

Worldliness is anything that draws us away from God. It can be something as trivial as a television or a newspaper or the radio, or a car, or the home, or a job, or an attitude. But we are in wartime, and we have to remember that in wartime we travel light. Sometimes Christians do need a stark reminder that they are not at home in this world, they are just passing through. We must get our priorities right. If we do not, we will be the church at play, not the church at war.

Dealing with wrong attitudes

So the Israelites were getting ready on the plain to go to war. After three days, the officers went throughout the camp, stirring the people up, and giving them orders. 'When you see the ark of the covenant of the LORD your God,' they said, 'and the priests, who are Levites, carrying it, you are to move out from your positions and follow it. Then you will know which way to go, since you have never been this way before' (3:3-4).

These officers were probably not only military leaders,

but religious leaders as well. In the ancient world, the religious and the political/military were often combined. They would try to encourage the Israelites in their religious devotion.

No doubt they would have come across *many different* attitudes in the camp. Some would be impatient to get going. Others would be more laid-back; next year would be a good time for an attack. There were those who would be scared and not sure what they wanted. Still others would be thinking that lives would be lost in this attack, and consequently were worried, tense and anxious. But the officers went round the camp listening to people, telling them what was going to happen, keeping them up to date, sharing with them the concerns of the leadership, making sure that they understood that the battle was about to take place, and moving them on to the attack.

The focus of the officers' message was the ark of the covenant, a fairly large box in which the stones on which were written the Ten Commandments were placed, along with Aaron's rod and a sample of manna. It was very sacred, a symbol of God's holy and almighty presence.

The first thing the officers did for the people was to point them away from their moods, their fears, their own feelings, away from their own needs, to a living powerful God, symbolized in the ark of the covenant. The officers were saying, 'Look to God for victory tomorrow! Don't look to yourselves! Don't look inside, because your moods will betray you, your fears will overwhelm you, you will be defeated by them.'

The ark of the covenant would be going ahead of them through the Jordan. God was encouraging the people not to see a human victory, although they must play their part, but to look to him to go on ahead of them, preparing the way, clearing the ground. They were to expect a miraculous intervention from God.

I believe that one of the problems with the church is that we forget too easily that we are in the miracle business. In other words, nothing happens without a miracle. We need to be looking for God to be at work. The church does not grow except by a miracle; people are not born again except by a miracle. Sometimes we get so earthbound, we forget to look for the touch of the Almighty.

I remember reading an amazing story about a so-called miracle. Flying a private plane over Los Angeles an 80-year-old pilot had a sudden heart attack and died at the controls. Without a moment's hesitation, 69-year-old Charles Law, who had never flown a plane before, took over the wheel of the Cessna 150 and, guided in by air traffic control, landed it safely. 'I don't know how he did it,' said police sergeant John Cameron, who led a convoy of ambulances and fire engines to the air strip. 'It was a miracle.' It certainly was. After he landed, Charles Law had to be led from the plane. He was blind.

Sometimes we look to God for a miracle, but can be too satisfied with the little things in life. When God blesses us in a little way, we rightly thank him, but can fail to see that there may be an even bigger miracle just waiting to be released as our faith goes on trusting and asking.

Yet in the face of the absence of miracles, we must go on trusting God. Miracles do not always happen. Sometimes people are prayed for and they are not healed; at times they seem to get worse and we do not understand why that is.

Faith is not dependent on whether or not God works a miracle.
It is dependent on God.

But God wants to move, and that is why this incident from
the history of Israel is so critical to us. It puts the focus away
from the thousands of people, the massive army, on to the ark
of the covenant of God. The ark, in and of itself, was nothing;
it was unpretentious, relatively small and not very ornate.
The box was only a symbol of the God to whom it pointed.
And we are pointed beyond ourselves, beyond our religion,
even beyond the Bible, to God himself; we do not worship
the Bible, we worship God. And seeing him, the miracles for
which we pray become all the more possible.

New beginnings by God's grace

The ark of the covenant would guide the people of Israel into
new territory. True, they had been in Shittim before, and they
knew what it was like. Maybe they were keen to leave in
case there was a repetition of the earlier failure. But once out
of Shittim, they were in places that they had never been in
before, and had to look to God to guide them.

All believers' lives can be like this! The thing about each
new day is that we have never been through it before. Many
believers are not where they ought to be in their Christian lives,
and I include myself among them. One reason for this is that
basically we see the future as a direct repeat of the past, and
therefore we are bound by it.

Take the Christian who has always had a bad temper and
nothing he does deals with it; it has followed him through life
and taints the future. Or take another Christian who has a
problem with gossip or negative comments; it grips her soul
and she just cannot seem to shake it off. But just because it

happened yesterday does not mean it must happen tomorrow. *That's the biblical principle of discontinuity.*

The coming week at work is like none that you have ever lived through before. That is not a threat, nor is it a promise; it is just a fact. It is a glorious fact, however, because it is so freeing. Today, we can choose to be different from what we have been up to now. We can choose today to look to God to make us different and not to have our past replicated in the future.

The Israelites trod on virgin territory, they walked across the plain towards the Jordan ravine below, and every step was fresh territory. And we walk into our future, every step unknown. We do not know what tomorrow will bring, good or bad, blessing or disaster. But as we look to God in Jesus Christ, we see our Saviour dying on the cross for us, we see an empty grave, we see him risen from the dead, gloriously ascended into heaven. And we can look inside ourselves, not to our own resources but to the Spirit living within us, God in our lives, who guides us on into the future. I do not know how to go into the future, except I go looking to Jesus, and serving him.

Some commentators think that the people were not to come close to the ark because it was a holy thing. That may have been one reason, but I think it is not the only one. Instead I think it is a practical command because if all the thousands of people were to be able to see the ark, then there had to be a certain distance between it and the people in front.

Preparation by consecration

Then Joshua told the people, 'Consecrate yourselves, for tomorrow the LORD will do amazing things among you' (3:5). When God wants to lead his people out of a period of confusion and bewilderment into a period of security and knowledge, they have to consecrate themselves.

There are two factors here worth noting: a *spiritual* attitude that resulted in *physical* activity.

The physical activity of consecration involved abstaining from sexual activity, washing in a particular way, and observing other religious rituals including prayers of various kinds. The spiritual activity, however, is the more important.

The way to see amazing things happen in the church is not just by abstaining from sexual activity, washing more regularly and having prayers at various times of the day. The Bible does say that certain things done physically do have a clear bearing on our spiritual activity, which is why fasting is a source of spiritual power. In 1 Corinthians 7:5 Paul says that in order for Christians to give themselves to prayer, it can be appropriate to abstain from sexual activity for a while.

But the key is not the physical activities, it is the spiritual attitudes. Joshua does not say: 'Consecrate yourselves, because tomorrow you're going to do some really great things.' No, he says that if the Israelites consecrate themselves, God will do great things. It is our responsibility to consecrate ourselves and it is God's responsibility to do the amazing things. I find that a very fair exchange of labour.

Like the Israelites of Joshua's day, we are called to consecrate ourselves, to sanctify ourselves. If we want God to do amazing things, we, as the people of God, must *together* be holy. That is not to say that God will not do amazing things until every single one of his people is holy. If God had to wait for that there would be no miracles until the Second Coming. There is not a church, there is not a house group, there is not an organization, there is not an individual, there is not a family that is totally consecrated to God. So waiting for that is only a waste of time.

Fortunately God asks us instead, as he asked the Israelites, to take a step on the road to consecration. The tense of the verb is the present continuous: 'Go about the task of consecrating yourself, and don't stop consecrating yourself.' Keep on being consecrated and then when you do, you will see the Lord go on doing amazing things.

Some of us need to move closer towards the goal of consecration before God will do the amazing things he wants to. As believers we are called to be more consecrated to him, to be more holy, to seek his face, to learn to love and to adore him, to want him in all his splendour and beauty, to want him above everything else. That is what consecration is; total commitment to him, with Jesus not just resident but also president in control.

Holiness is not a matter of what you do not do; it is not a matter of using a certain kind of language, or going to certain places. It is not wearing an intense expression in worship, it is not singing in a special way, it is not reading your Bible in a particular way. Those things may be the physical results, but what is paramount is the spiritual attitude of consecrating ourselves to God.

5

Risky leadership
Joshua 3:6-17

Joshua, under God's instruction, told the priests who carried the ark of the covenant, 'When you reach the edge of the Jordan's water, go and stand in the river.' The river was in flood, it being the time of the spring harvest. God was requiring the priests to take on the role of active, risky leadership, in addition to their normal function of interpreting the Old Testament law. Similarly, it is important today to have leaders who know what it is to take risks for God and not be afraid to move on. When such people take risks with God, Christians will follow them, and will honour the faith of the leaders God has called.

When organization is not enough
I wonder what the priests felt like, stepping into the water? They must have been a bit nervous, but until they got their feet wet, God did not work the miracle of faith. One of the problems of the church of Jesus today is that often, before we will do anything, we want it all worked out, right down to the minute details.

Yes, there is a need for careful planners in the church, after all, administration is one of the gifts of the Spirit. We need to be thinking carefully through all we do. Slap-dash efforts ought to have no part in the things of the church.

But there comes a point when organization itself is not

enough. We must recognize that the church is not like a club or an organization. The church operates best when it operates at the level of the Spirit. In other words, it operates best when it operates at the level of the supernatural.

Let me repeat that the church is not against the organization and administration that are needed to run it and prevent it from becoming sloppy and third-rate. But God does not organize his way into a miracle, and we cannot organize him into a miracle. We must work as if God is going to do very little, but we must have faith to believe that he is going to do everything.

After having done every thing we can do in preparation, having consulted with others, and having thought and prayed and planned and worked, God does say sometimes, 'Step into the Jordan.' When God says that, we have to get our feet wet.

There are Christian laymen and leaders whose entire Christian lives are in the normal, in the ordinary. There may be no doubt that they have been saved and will spend eternity with God in perfect joy, but their earthly lives are marked by a great reluctance to step out beyond the known, to where God calls us to take risks for him.

If we live like this, we will miss out on the spiritual dimension of Christian living. Yes, we may make mistakes, but there are going to be times when, by acting in this way, we consecrate ourselves to the Lord and will see him do amazing things.

This step of faith is needed too in human relationships. I prepared as carefully as possible for my marriage. Before I proposed to Jan, I thought very carefully about what it was that I was about to get into. I thought about her and her gifts and abilities. I considered what it would mean to take a Texan to England to live, and all the adjustment it would involve for her. I felt sure that it was what God wanted. But it was a dimension that demanded a step of faith. And it has been amply rewarded!

Just as we need that element of faith in all human relations, so it is in our relationship with God. Many people, who are asking questions about becoming a Christian, struggle with the intellectual arguments for a long time. Then they realize their finite mind will never understand everything there is to understand, and that there will always be another question. And until a step of faith is taken, the experience of God's power and love will not happen. This is not an attack on the use of the mind. But it is a reminder that the mind can only take us so far in the things of God.

Spiritual sanity

Joshua said to the Israelites, 'Come here and listen to the words of the LORD your God. This is how you will know that the living God is among you... See, the ark of the covenant of the Lord of all the earth will go into the Jordan ahead of you... And as soon as the priests who carry the ark of the LORD – the Lord of all the earth – set foot in the Jordan, the water flowing downstream will be cut off and stand up in a heap' (3:9-11).

When the priests stood in the river, Joshua told the Israelites the words of the Lord their God. The response of the Israelites to these words is what makes the miracle possible and the faith realistic.

The difference between faith on the one hand, and straightforward lunacy on the other, is that the faithful are responding to the Word of God, while the 'lunatics' are usually responding to their own feelings in the guise of 'a word from the Lord'.

The faithful demand to listen to the Word of God. In our church services we need consistently to have time to listen to God. And we need to have time in our private lives to hear what God is saying.

What God says about the way forward is absolutely critical. In the spiritual life, as Joshua discovered here on the edge of the Jordan, there are two aspects to victory. The first is a divine component: come and listen to the Word of the Lord; and the second is the human component: go and get your feet wet.

The trouble is that all too often we put up a divide between the two requirements. Some Christians seem incredibly holy and spend all their time vaguely listening for words from God. But when it comes down to getting their hands dirty, or, to use the Joshua metaphor, getting their feet wet, they are not involved in kingdom business. They say, 'Let's sit down and listen to God's Word, let's rest in him, let's sit with an open Bible in times of quiet.' But they may not warm so well to 'Shut your Bibles, stop praying, and get out there!'

There are others who are grubbing around in kingdom business, working all the hours God sends, but who are not necessarily doing what God wants them to do, because they have not had a word from him about it.

We need both these types of Christian in the church as different people will emphasize different things. And as long as the contemplative do not look down their noses at the activists, or *vice versa*, it will be fine. As long as we hear from God together, and do what he is calling us to do, things will prosper.

The Israelites could have sat on the edge of Jordan listening to words from God and singing choruses for twenty years and would never have crossed the Jordan unless someone had said, 'Go!' But they would have all drowned in the Jordan, if they had just gone when they felt like it.

When the time was right, Joshua instructed the people to choose one man from each of the twelve tribes to go on ahead with the priests. Then he speaks these remarkable words: 'As soon as the priests who carry the ark of the LORD – the Lord of all the earth – step into the Jordan, the water flowing downstream will be cut off...' He reminds them that God is the Lord of all the earth. This name implies his creative genius. It means that the flow of a river in full flood is entirely at his disposal, and incredible as it may seem, in terms of God's power, it is nothing. He can deal easily with the flow of a river. He is not just the Lord of one of these tribes, he is not just the Lord of a geographical area or of a particular season, as many thought in those times. He is the Lord of all the earth.

And so, 'the priests who carried the ark of the covenant of the LORD stood firm on dry ground in the middle of the Jordan, while all Israel passed by until the whole nation had completed the crossing on dry ground' (3:17).

6

That the earth might know
Joshua 4:1-5:12

So the people of Israel crossed the Jordan safely and, once they had built a memorial of God's greatness, they prepared to fight. We read in verse 13: 'About forty thousand armed for battle crossed over before the LORD, to the plains of Jericho for war.' What I find thrilling in this incident is that the people of God change from being spectators in the wilderness to being participants in conquering a kingdom. Christians have the unique privilege of having been transferred from a kingdom which is full of darkness to one which is full of light. We are thereby given the right to wield the swords of light, so that darkness wherever it is found can be exposed and rooted out. Light can shine where once there was darkness in people's lives, in their circumstances and in other situations.

If we are not careful, however, it is possible to overdo the spiritual warfare metaphor in regard to Christian living, imagining warfare situations where they do not exist. Sometimes we blame Satan for things, when in reality the cause is our own stupidity. We should admit that and say sorry to God. But, Scripture is quite clear that Christians are in a spiritual warfare situation, and we need to cross the Jordan, metaphorically speaking, and be involved in fighting the battle.

However, there are some Christians who, instead of pressing on to fight, prefer to slip back over the Jordan, as it were, back to meandering through the wilderness, making no impact on the giants in Canaan. Others, who do not to go back over the Jordan, are content to settle down alongside the equivalent of the twelve great stones we read of in Joshua 4:9, and say, 'Look what God has done, isn't it great! My word, what a lovely memorial!' But the purpose of the memorial was to point others to what God had done, not to sit and admire the stones that had been erected.

We can learn much from the people of Israel at the time of Joshua. Many of the features that marked them out are important for us, as Christians, today: they were united, there was a reality to their relationship with God and they were grateful.

1. Unity. The people of God demonstrated a real togetherness at this point of their history, when they were crossing the Jordan and preparing for war. They were facing a powerful enemy, secure in fortified cities. Canaan was flowing with milk and honey, but it was also the home of great giants. To achieve the victory, they needed to be strong people bound together.

It is so easy to be complacent and self-satisfied in the church in the West today. Perhaps if we were put on a warfare footing, it would breed the sense of togetherness. People in a warfare situation are bound together.

2. Reality in their relationship with God. Sometimes I wonder if the church in Britain, in singing its songs and enjoying its worship experiences, has so trivialised the glorious truths of the faith that it has forgotten that it is in a warfare situation.

Often we sing words and we have no idea what we are

singing. For example, *'Here I am, wholly available'* – if one church member in five hundred believed that, we would have a revolution.

Let me make a confession as a preacher, which any who have been in leadership will relate to. It is much easier to preach about holiness than it is to live a holy life. It is much easier to preach about prayer than to pray. It is much easier to preach about being filled with the Spirit than it is to be filled with the Spirit. I feel the inconsistency in my own life as I struggle to both preach and live in the same way.

As the people of God, we have to live out in practice what we say we believe in theory, and let the gospel affect our moods, our attitudes, our behaviour, our words and the way we live our lives.

3. Gratitude. God was calling the Israelites to move over the Jordan, to the inheritance he had planned for them. And on the way, there were those piles of stones. Every time in the future when someone would pass the pile and ask, 'What's that?', they would be told, 'That reminds us of what God did in the past. We would never have made it here without him.'

Sometimes people have little mementoes in their homes to remind them of times when God worked powerfully. There are verses from songs or hymns that are very precious to Jan and I, because they came at critical moments in our lives and whenever we hear those words sung, we smile at each other and say, 'That was a key moment. We praise God for what he did.'

I long that you will have many occasions in your life to erect real or imaginary stones or little things that trigger your memory so that your whole life is a constant exclamation of

'Look what God has done!' I would not be where I am if it were not for the work of God. Neither would you. Look at what God has done for you!

And of course, the Lord's Supper is the supreme example of a 'Tell what God has done' sign. It is a visual aid that the church has been using for two thousand years to remind us of Jesus' death on the cross and resurrection.

The twelve stones in the middle of the river did not accidentally roll out of the river bed and form a pile. There was a deliberate activity by the people. It would not have been easy to lift these boulders. And in the Lord's Supper we are to make a special step of saying, 'Lord, thank you for what you have done in my life. I actively reach out to take the bread and the wine as a sign of my gratitude for what you have done for me.'

Seeing God's power

In 4:24 we read, 'He [dried up the Jordan before you] so that all the peoples of the earth might know that the hand of the LORD is powerful and so that you [the Israelites] might always fear the LORD your God.' This verse is not only a summary verse, it is also a bridging verse, tying the events of chapters 4 and 5 together. 'Now when all the Amorite kings west of the Jordan and all the Canaanite kings along the sea coast, heard how the LORD had dried up the Jordan before the Israelites until we had crossed over, their hearts sank, and they no longer had the courage to face the Israelites' (5:1).

In the ancient world, unless you were a dictator like Nebuchadnezzar, it was very hard to maintain control over a large area. It was more common for the land to be divided into smaller areas, each with its own ruler, like in ancient

Britain when the people were governed by barons and lords.

The Amorite and Canaanite kings had all sorts of gods – a god for each season, and so on. They had heard reports that the God of Israel was powerful, but suddenly they heard a rumour that he had dried up a river bed. They knew that their gods could not do that. The miracle was a signal to them of the power of the living God.

Today, exactly the same thing pertains. Whenever God moves in his miraculous power, it sends a shudder through the powers that be, whether the demonic forces or the powers of the world. I have spoken to people who are not Christians about someone who has become a Christian. They have seen this person's life transformed before their eyes and they have been unable to explain how the transformation has taken place. And it has sent a kind of shudder through them.

We should pray for demonstrations of God's power, so that the world will see that the church is more than just a holy club, more than a gathering of nice people who help each other a bit, but that it is a place where God reigns.

During the wilderness wanderings of the Israelites, God demonstrated his presence among them by the Shekinah glory that hovered over them. As Christians we gather together not only to sing and pray, but in order for the glory of God to descend among us, so that we will sense his living, incredible power. It is this that makes believers different; not that we are better than others in some way, but that God is present with us.

Fear the LORD your God

The miracle of holding back the Jordan was not just a demonstration of God's power for the world, it was that the

people of God might continue to fear the Lord their God
(4:24).

The fear of God is a consistent biblical theme, perhaps
more obvious in the Old Testament than in the New Testament.
From Genesis to Malachi the prevailing theme is the fear of
the Lord, who is awesome and powerful. The passion of the
New Testament seems to be that God is approachable. These
two themes, however, are not contradictory, they simply relate
to different aspects of God's divine nature.

The Old Testament focuses on the awe, respect and honour
due to the glorious Creator God who kept his people safe
from their enemies and ultimately brought them into the
Promised Land. But the New Testament teaches that Christians
are not to fear God in the sense of being anxious or terrified.

It is similar to a good family relationship. When children
are growing up, parents develop a relationship with them
which involves a certain element of fear. I do not mean a
dreadful fear, but there has to be a healthy respect for parents.
The children have to believe that if parents command
something, the consequences for disobedience are serious.

God wants believers to remember always that they are the
church and that he is God. They should not decide what they
ought to be doing as a church, and then give their plans to
God. Rather they should ask God what he wants them to do.

In our culture we all come under pressure not to fear or
respect anything or anyone. Authority figures of various levels
are mocked. The whole rise of alternative comedy is an
interesting sign that now there are no areas which cannot be
mocked. There is no question that twenty years ago God, Jesus,
religion and the church would not have been the objects of
abusive attack. But today the media and some of the alternative

comedians are guilty of doing so. The name of Jesus is not respected as it once was; God is not honoured as he once was.

Sadly that attitude invades the church. Believers watch the same television, read the same newspapers, live in the same world as non-Christians, and it is inevitable that we absorb some values of the prevailing world-view. And so the love, honour and awe of the living God we should feel can be weakened because he is diminished in our eyes. Today's generation has elevated mankind and diminished the deity and many believers are impoverished as a result. But God will do the miraculous to restore a rightful fear of him.

Painful restoration

When the Israelites were forbidden to enter Canaan and punished by forty years of wilderness wandering, there was a sense in which they were rejected as God's people. The rejection was not permanent, but their relationship with God was on hold for thirty-eight years until a whole unbelieving generation had died out.

Circumcision was a special sign that the Israelites were chosen by God and set apart for his purposes. But it was not appropriate in their state of disobedience, and so the children born during those years in the wilderness had not been circumcised. When the Lord told Joshua to circumcise these men, to reinstate the ritual, it was a sign of their coming back to God. This episode is recounted in Joshua 5:1-8.

Circumcision was a painful and debilitating experience. The fighting men would have been incapacitated for several days, and unfit for fighting until their wounds were healed. The Israelites would have been vulnerable to enemy attack during that time. Scripture actually records another incident where men were circumcised and their enemies took them by surprise before their wounds were healed. Unable to put up much of a fight, they were wiped out (see Genesis 34).

In this instance, however, God had so ordered events that there was no threat of a surprise attack. Verse 1 of chapter 5 helps to make sense of this. We read that the inhabitants of Canaan were too terrified of God's power to attack the Israelites. Thus the very vulnerable people were safe during this period of weakness. But the weakness was a consequence of obedience. I was thrilled to note that a vulnerable people are protected when they are obedient.

This is what faith is all about: putting ourselves on a human level, by being obedient, yet recognizing God's protection when we step out for him. That is what happened to the children of Israel. They made a commitment to do the right thing, and when they did so, God protected them from enemy attack. The right thing was the renewal of their covenant.

One of the most frustrating experiences of modern life is when you phone someone and the switch board puts you on hold. You are totally powerless until someone at the other end picks up the phone and starts talking.

God had not wanted to stop the relationship with the Israelites, but they put him on hold. The act of circumcision then was, in a sense, their clearing the switchboard and saying, 'God, we're open to you now. We will do what you tell us to do. We are ready to listen, we are ready to obey and we won't hold you off any longer.'

There are individuals, including those in positions of leadership, whose relationship with God is not what it should be because of sin and rebellion in their lives. People in this situation could be described as having put God on hold. They are not ready to hear from him because he may say something they do not want to hear. How many of us need to have what is wrong cut away from us, in a kind of spiritual circumcision. It is a painful experience, but by it we are put right with God.

So the people of Israel were returned to relationship with God, their disobedience was forgiven and the Lord said to Joshua, 'Today I have rolled away the reproach of Egypt from you' (5:9).

Celebrating the Passover

Following this momentous episode, on the evening of the fourteenth day of the month, while camped at Gilgal on the plains of Jericho, the Israelites celebrated the Passover. The day after the Passover they ate some of the produce of the land – unleavened bread and roasted grain. The manna, which God had provided for them throughout their wilderness wanderings, stopped the day after they ate the produce of the land. This was a sign that normal service was being resumed.

For years they were vulnerable and had nowhere to turn. They were in a desert place where food was extremely scarce, especially for their kind of numbers. God had to provide food for them miraculously. But when they reached the land of milk and honey, God withdrew the supernatural provision and told them to get on with the task of being obedient.

Some believers whom God has bailed out again and again from difficult situations have become complacent about it. One day, God will say, 'Because I love you, I've bailed you out for the last time. I am giving the provision for you to work it out yourself. For you to be a blessing, you are to get on with the job of doing what I have given you to do.'

The Israelites could celebrate the Passover because they had been circumcised, and were now listening to God. The attitude of the children of Israel had changed from the wilderness-wandering mumble-grumble attitude, to one of praise and gratitude on the verge of conquest. A grateful people celebrated a meal together, thanking God for what he had done for them in setting them free.

7

Encountering the Divine Leader
Joshua 5:13-15

Joshua had proved what a capable and godly leader he was
in the way he brought Israel across the Jordan. The next, great
challenge to his abilities as leader, was to capture the fortified
city of Jericho. Perhaps the size of the task left him feeling
broken and despairing. He wanted to be brave, but was
apprehensive at the prospect of what was before him. So, it
would seem that Joshua went on a personal scouting mission
to check out Jericho.

Imagine the scene. Joshua is hiding in some undergrowth
looking up at Jericho when suddenly he becomes aware of
another presence nearby. Looking around, he sees a man with
a drawn sword. That is a threatening position. Being a soldier
Joshua leaps to his feet to confront this stranger and to discover
whose side he is on.

The stranger's reply must have staggered Joshua: 'Neither,'
he replied, 'but as commander of the army of the LORD I have
come' (verse 14). Joshua realized in whose presence he was,
and fell face down to the ground in reverence. He realised
that he was before God.

What happened here was either a theophany (an
appearance of the living God himself in human form) or an
angel of God sent directly from God to give Joshua a message.
The only appropriate response was for Joshua to fall flat on
his face in the sight of the visitor and say, 'Why have you
come to me?'

Joshua was probably trying to work out a human strategy to conquer Jericho, but God's answer was a divine strategy (we will come back to the details of this strategy later). It is a reminder to us that in the face of all of our humanity, God often has another way which short-circuits all our schemes. Human beings are incredibly limited. We are always facing our 'Jerichos'; for example, How am I going to cope with this situation at work? How am I going to cope with this family issue? How am I going to cope with these worries about my health? What does the future hold? The problems can seem like a huge fortified city.

The world today is a place of continual and significant change. All sorts of problems keep throwing themselves up for us, as Christians, to think about and work through. The massive complexity of modern life confronts with an apparently simple faith in God. We are faced not just with personal dilemmas, but with massive ethical, philosophical and moral dilemmas.

We know that our finite human minds can only get so far in solutions to these difficult problems. At the end of the day, whether the issue is a personal 'Jericho', or a cultural, philosophical 'Jericho', the ultimate answer is not in our strategies but in the commander of the army of the Lord of hosts. We need to be open to divine resources. God has solutions beyond our wildest dreams. When we acknowledge that he knows and we do not, we suddenly get in the right position: flat on our faces before God.

Standing on holy ground
The commander of the Lord's army told Joshua, 'Take off your sandals for the place where you are standing is holy.' It

reminds us of the time when God spoke to Moses out of the burning bush, when he called him to be leader of the people of Israel (Exodus 3). Both Moses and Joshua were told to take off their sandals for the place where they stood was holy ground. Two consecutive leaders of the children of Israel were both told exactly the same thing in their commissioning service. The commissioning from God's messengers, whether by the burning bush, or the soldier assessing Jericho, is a commissioning out of holiness. What set Joshua and Moses apart as chosen leaders of their day and generation, was their encounter with a holy God.

If we want to be useful in God's service, if we want to be those who make a difference in our place of work or home, if we want to be God's leaders, we will need an encounter with his holiness in order to be that kind of person. There is no short cut around this.

Some people seem only to want to get zapped by God's power. In some cases, the preaching on the fulness of the Spirit has resulted in devastating results, because it has brought power into the lives of people who were unable to cope with it. The key to Christian leadership is not just power and authority, but holiness as well.

Joshua and Moses were called to live a holy life. Both were commanded to take off their sandals for they were on holy ground. The imagery is a sort of reverent quietness, where you take off your sandals and tiptoe around in awe, waiting on tenterhooks for what might happen. Holiness is not a matter of what you do or do not do, it is an attitude.

When I was growing up, my grandparents, who were very strict about a whole range of things, defined holiness in terms of behaviour. I still remember being told as a young child that certain kinds of behaviour were unacceptable. Holiness was often defined in negative terms about what one did not do. The Bible, on the other hand, defines holiness in terms of an encounter with God, as an inner thing. Jesus sets us free to be pure and holy because of something inside.

Of course, certain places ought to be avoided, particularly when we are new Christians, because they are places of temptation. But holiness is not about places one cannot go to, or words one does not use, or things one does not do. Neither is holiness defined in terms of religious observance. Holiness is an encounter with the living God who wants us to be pure on the inside.

On God's side

When Joshua said to the commander, 'Are you on our side or our enemy's?', the commander replied, 'Neither. You've got it wrong, Joshua. You are on my side. I call the shots, not you.'

There was a period in British history where the implication was that God was an Englishman. Most cultures created a god in their own image, and the god of the Englishman was nice and gentle, and, being British, quietly reserved. We as a nation tended to believe that God was on our side.

Christians love to have God on their side. Churches can be very arrogant sometimes and believe that God is with them; he might be with other churches, but if he is, he is only there occasionally! We are on very dangerous territory when we believe that.

Sometimes I am called on to arbitrate between two Christians who have fallen out. Often one will state: 'God is on my side in this.' If that is the case, there is no point in having any further discussion! However, it is more usual for the statement to be used in the misguided attempt to bolster a feeble argument.

When our arguments seem unconvincing, we have a tendency to drag God into it in a way that is barely short of blasphemous. We are in great danger when we just assume that God is on our side.

Joshua and Moses were commissioned by an encounter with holiness. If today's leaders want to serve God they will have to have a similar encounter. They need to meet the holy God, because unless the ego, the self, has been disinfected by this encounter, they will simply be serving God in fleshly terms. They need to be in submission, flat on their faces, before the Commander, the Lord of hosts, because in every 'Jericho' they will face, they will only be successful as they know the wisdom of the Commander rather than their own human wisdom.

8

Destroying the stronghold of Jericho
Joshua 6:1-27

The children of Israel were poised to attack Jericho. Inside the city fear reigned, because of the massive horde that surrounded it. The city of Jericho was small by today's standards, nothing like as big as London. It was a small provincial town, with a population of less than 20,000, but strategically placed.

Perhaps Joshua, after hearing the Lord's plan, which involved lots of marching round Jericho following priests playing musical instruments, was waiting for plan B, which would be to ram the gates and scale the walls. But God did not have plan B.

Here is the scenario. It may well have taken less than an hour to walk all the way round the walls. For six mornings, the Israelites were to assemble early and walk round the city. Then on the seventh day, it may have been the Sabbath, they were to do it seven times. This was a costly act of obedient worship, far more costly in some ways than to attack by the more conventional method.

There were two things to which they were exposed here. Firstly, it was *dangerous*. Normally when an army attacks a city it stays out of sight for as long as possible, for the element of surprise is important. We can imagine how the inhabitants of Jericho might have felt on looking over the wall at this huge line of people walking silently round the city, following the ark and the musicians. I suspect they were confused and unable to imagine what the Israelites were going to do next. But the Israelites, once again, were in a vulnerable situation through their obedience. They could be seen, and presumably they could be shot at with bows and arrows or have spears and stones hurled at them. But they were under strict instructions to walk round the city.

Secondly, they were *exposed to ridicule*. We can imagine the people of Jericho laughing. After all they had never been attacked by a trumpet before! Ridicule is something that we see so much of in our own culture. Christians in many situations are exposed to ridicule from people who do not understand a different lifestyle. Today Christianity seems as absurd as conquering a city by walking round it.

But the divine principle is just the same for modern believers as it was for Joshua. The Lord gives the strength, the power and the authority to cope with ridicule. The power of Christianity does not reside in our ability, but in our availability to God's ability. And as we are open to his incredible power, so we cope with the ridicule that is bound to come when we stand up for something that is right.

Ridicule was heaped on God's people all the way through the Old Testament period. They were constantly being mocked for believing in an invisible God, for in the ancient world everybody could see their god.

In our own culture, too, seeing is believing. Because Christians cannot say what their God looks like they are open to ridicule. We do not seem rational or reasonable or sensible. Yet the Spirit realm is rational, and sensible, and, what's more, is the power that runs the universe. God, although we cannot see him, is the ultimate reality.

God's victory

It was the ultimate reality of the living God who sent the people walking around Jericho. He did this in order to make sure they understood that he was in control and the city was going to be given to them by him and not by their numerical strength. Similarly, as we are exposed to ridicule, we need to recognize that God's power is with us.

In reality it was only a little thing that God asked them to do. To walk round the city, even seven times on the final day – well, that was not hard.

But it would have been tiring, especially on the last day. When the Israelites were absolutely shattered at the end of several hours of marching, God says, 'Now the battle starts!' This was another device to show that God was going to win the victory not the Israelites.

> Some scholars have suggested that there was not a miracle here at all. What happened, according to them, was that the continual marching loosened the foundation, and so when the Israelites shouted loudly on the last day, the energy in the loudness of the shout knocked the walls down!!?

In our Christian lives the key victories of faith are not won at the point of the big challenge, they are won in the small instances where, year in year out, in the mundane and the ordinary, we are obedient to the living God. Then as we learn obedience over the months and years, when we face the big challenges of faith we can rise to them.

Far too often, we long for the thrill of the big step of faith, when actually God calls us to be faithful in the small things. Joshua would not have had the faith to conquer Jericho in

God's way if he had not been obedient in the small things through all the years of the wilderness wandering. And neither would Jericho have been captured if the Israelites had not obeyed God and walked around the city for seven days.

Keeping at it

Put yourself in the position of one of these ordinary fighting men. Having been told what was likely to happen, what would you be doing as day after day you marched round the walls, not allowed to say anything? After the second or third day you would, no doubt, have been looking for signs of decay in the walls, for some little gesture from God, some indication that this ridiculous activity was paying off, and that God was generally loosening the bricks.

There is an important principle here. God did not demand that they simply walk round the city once before the walls came down. No, they had to walk around thirteen times, with apparently nothing happening, and then the walls fell down. The principle is that we need to persist even when we can see no results.

There is a parallel here with praying for people to become Christians. What tends to happen is that people are very resistant to God, and the more you pray for them and share your faith with them, the more antagonistic they become to the Christian faith. Until, over a matter of days, and I have seen it over hours, all resistance crumbles away in a moment and they are born again. And I think, 'How did that happen? A week ago he was an enemy to Christian things, now suddenly he is saved?'

What I could not see was that while I was praying, although the person's facade remained utterly unchanged, God was doing an incredible work inside him. Then there came the moment when God worked a miracle and the person was saved. But the truth is that for weeks, months or even years God had been working in that person's life by his Spirit.

As Christians, our work and our efforts are already undermining the foundations of sin and Satan in people's lives. But when we feel we are getting nowhere we can give up too soon. Victory, however, follows a marathon and not a sprint. Winning the world for Christ demands a long-term strategy, not a short-term thrashing about with lots of energy trying to make something happen, assuming that we are going to change an individual overnight.

Yet we expect non-Christians, after we have shared the gospel with them and prayed for them for a week or so, to say, 'You'll never believe this but I've made a complete fool of myself for my entire life! I've just changed my mind about everything I've ever believed. That conversation we had has completely turned my life around. You have convinced me utterly.'

People do not respond like that. Instead, we need the patience and faith of Joshua, walking round the city time after time, committed to see God's victory taking place. We need to be able to see with the eye of faith something going on behind the walls that human eyes cannot see.

When it is all added up, the greatest influence on the world, from God's point of view, may well be not the prominent people who grab the limelight, but the men and women who faithfully serve and love and pray and never give up. Those are the people who ultimately will see 'Jericho' fall, as they walk with God.

The walls fall down

On the seventh day, when they had marched round the city seven times, Joshua commanded the people to, 'Shout! For the LORD has given you the city!' In those two phrases, we find the difference between stupidity and faith. If you would like to know what stupidity is, why do you not go out and walk round the outside of your house seven times and then shout loudly at it. By that time your neighbours will be twitching the curtains to see what is going on. Nothing, of course, will happen because the second phrase is not true for us as it was for the Israelites; we can shout all we like but God has not said the walls will fall down. So the shouting is of no consequence unless there is a promise from God to back it up.

The walls of Jericho probably began with a minor wall of roughly twelve feet in height, and then a very smooth, almost polished stone surface sloping at a very sharp angle up to a wall of probably another thirty feet beyond that. Obviously it was a well-fortified city.

There have been a number of discussions about what happened to Rahab's house. Did her house fall down as well? That question has perplexed Bible scholars over the years. There are number of options, and I will mention two.

Firstly, it is quite possible that when the walls fell down, one little piece of wall, where Rahab's house was did not fall down. Another suggestion is that it was only the higher wall that fell down, and her house was built on the lower wall.

Whatever actually happened, God preserved Rahab and her family because he honoured the promise that the spies had made.

Going back to the Israelites, I wonder what they shouted? It is interesting that Scripture does not actually tell us what they shouted. Perhaps 'Get down!' 'Fall down!' Or was it a glorious cheer in celebration of the victory of God: 'Praise God for his power!' 'Our God will do it!'

God honoured his promise to give them the city. But the key thing here is that men and women acted with faith on the basis of a word from God.

Some Christians have felt that God was calling them to take outrageous steps of faith. But when they stepped out they fell flat on their faces. Because of that negative experience they have become timid, faithless Christians. Other Christians, as they get older and wiser and more mature in their Christian experience, become more boring. Still others become more faithless, and, as the years go by, tend to preserve the *status quo*.

The key to faithful Christian living, whether you are 9, 19 or 90, is to hear a word from God and to act upon it in faith. And that is how it was with Joshua and the people of God. 'When the trumpet sounded, the people shouted, and at the sound of the trumpet, when the people gave a loud shout, the wall collapsed; so every man charged straight in and they took the city' (6:20).

The verse that follows this triumph is a very difficult one for modern readers to cope with: 'They devoted the city to the LORD and destroyed with the sword every living thing in it – men and women, young and old, cattle, sheep and donkeys.' In today's world, it is very difficult to imagine God wanting the wholesale destruction of men and women and animals. With our twentieth century views of the sanctity of life and our tolerance of other religions, it seems incredibly bloodthirsty. I will come back to this difficult subject in chapter 14.

What we need to remember is that the Old Testament has a great understanding of the awesome nature of the Holy God. We are often very casual about our view of sin, whereas in Old Testament times there was a fierce hatred of things that were wrong and anti-God. The church of Jesus in our nation has much to learn from the Israelites' concern for the name and the honour of God.

Moving on from the ruins

Joshua realized that before they could conquer the Promised Land, they had to conquer this key city. Until it was destroyed the Israelites would never possess the land. In its ruins there would always be a reminder of the power of God and his victory over evil.

There is a spiritual parallel here that is worth mentioning. Many believers have an area of their lives which needs to be given over to God's control. It might be a personality trait

---

In verse 26, Joshua pronounced a solemn oath: 'Cursed before the LORD is the man who undertakes to rebuild this city, Jericho.' The curse was a way of making sure that nothing would happen there again after Jericho was destroyed. About five hundred years after Joshua, during the reign of King Ahab, the city was rebuilt. 1 Kings 16:34 describes what happened: 'In Ahab's time, Hiel of Bethel rebuilt Jericho. He laid its foundations at the cost of his firstborn son Abiram, and he set up its gates at the cost of his youngest son Segub, in accordance with the word of the LORD spoken by Joshua son of Nun.'

which has been surrounded by huge walls to keep God out. It might be a bad temper; it might be a tendency to lie, or to gossip or to deceive; it might be an inner core of selfishness; it might be a relationship with someone. Whatever it is, its existence prevents God being in every area of our lives.

When we admit the sin and pray to him to deal with the problem, God breaks down the walls. All too often, however, we do not turn our backs on it and move on; instead we start to rebuild in the ruins. Like the ruins of Jericho were a reminder to the people of God's power, when he breaks down walls in our lives we need to pray for his strength to leave the rubble as a memorial, and to move on. God wants to set us free permanently.

9

Disobedience brings disaster
Joshua 7:1-15

In 1974 I was invited to go to Orlando, Florida, to take part in a mission. I had never been to the United States before. I flew from Manchester airport to Kennedy airport in New York. It was my first ever flight and it was really wonderful; there was no turbulence, no disruptions to the service, everybody was polite and the aircraft food was delicious.

The change over in New York went smoothly and the connection in Atlanta was on time. As the plane took off from Atlanta heading for Orlando, I leaned back in my seat and dreamed of all the things that I was going to experience in Florida. I thought of the sunshine and the beaches ...

Suddenly the plane started to make strange noises. I sat upright and rebuckled my seat belt (I did that to help the pilot!). The plane continued to make strange noises, and also to drop suddenly at intervals. In addition the stewardesses were rushing around. Then the captain's voice said, 'We are having an engine difficulty. We are going to try to make it back to Atlanta!'

You can imagine what this did to my quiet reflection on sun-drenched Florida. Thankfully we made it back safely. The problem was sorted out and three hours later it was time to re-board the same plane. Eventually we made it safely down to Orlando. But I remember the shock to my system caused by this interruption just when we thought everything was going so well.

Perhaps this shock was not unlike that experienced by the Israelites in Joshua 7. We read there of a frightening interruption to the ongoing progress that Joshua and the people of God had been taking for granted.

Joshua had sent out spies to assess the town of Ai. When they returned they reported that Ai would be defeated easily. Jericho had been no problem, after all. The spies were so confident of success that they said: 'Not all the people will have to go up against Ai. Send two or three thousand men to take it and do not weary all the people, for only a few men are there' (7:3). But things went badly wrong. They were routed by the men of Ai and were forced to retreat as far as the quarries. There the men of Ai killed thirty-six of them. 'At this the hearts of the people melted and became like water' (7:5). There has rarely been such a military turn-up for the books as what happened on this occasion.

A leader without power

Then Joshua tore his clothes and fell prostrate before the ark of the covenant. He cried out to God: 'Ah, Sovereign LORD, why did you ever bring this people across the Jordan to deliver us into the hands of the Amorites to destroy us? If only we had been content to stay on the other side of the Jordan! O Lord, what can I say, now that Israel has been routed by its enemies? The Canaanites and the other people of the country will hear about this and will surround us and wipe out our name from the earth. What then will you do for your great name?' (7:8-9).

This episode is reminiscent of the time when, thirty-eight years earlier, the spies returned from Canaan and informed Moses that defeat was inevitable:

> 'We can't attack those people; they are stronger than we are
> .... The land we explored devours those living in it. All the
> people we saw there are of great size' (Numbers 13:31-32).
>
> The people of Israel wept aloud and grumbled against
> Moses and Aaron, 'If only we had died in Egypt! Or in this
> desert! Why is the LORD bringing us to this land only to let
> us fall by the sword? ... Wouldn't it be better ... to go back
> to Egypt?' (Numbers 14:2-3).

Now it is Joshua's turn to be fearful and terrified because his
plans had crumbled and things were not turning out as he felt
they should.

These two episodes are a reminder that there will be times
when our plans will fail, when what we want above anything
else does not happen. Everything can be going really well in
our lives, then all of a sudden things begin to go wrong. This
can be in terms of employment, perhaps, or relationships or
health.

We see Joshua here wallowing in self-pity. His primary
concern is not the children of Israel, but himself, his leadership,
how will he look to all these people.

God, however, is blunt with Joshua. To those who are
damaged, or despairing, God speaks his care and love,
assuring of his constant presence. But to those who, like Joshua
here, are self-piteous, moaning about God and about other
believers, God says, as he said to Joshua, 'Get up! Why are
you lying on the ground like this? It is time for action. Sin has
occurred and I want you to go and sort it out.'

It is important to understand that this passage is not saying
that whenever failure occurs, there must be sin in our lives.
All too often when there is a problem in a church, people
tend, very judgmentally, to look for the sin. When there is

still not the blessing they expected, they single someone else out as the culprit. That kind of judgmentalism is not what this passage is about.

But it is a word for some who are wallowing in their own shame at their failures and mistakes. People in this situation can sometimes get to like it, because it brings them constantly before God. But to such God says, 'Get up!'

God revealed to Joshua that Israel had sinned and had broken the agreement with God. Someone had violated the covenant and stolen 'devoted things'. The Lord continued: 'That is why the Israelites cannot stand against their enemies; they turn their backs and run because they have been made liable to destruction. I will not be with you any more unless you destroy whatever among you is devoted to destruction' (7:12).

God then told Joshua to gather the people, to purify them and get them ready to serve God.

A leader in despair

Imagine the Israelites seeing Joshua down on the ground. They probably wondered what had happened to their incredible leader. They knew about his prowess. How weak and pitiful he seemed now, belying his great reputation.

Very few can live up to their reputations. Joshua certainly could not live up to his reputation as a great commander, in fact, at this point he was rather pathetic. I have found this so challenging. Often Christians, leaders and lay people, are very concerned about how they appear to one another. But our main concern should be how we appear to God.

Twice God tells Joshua to get up. God did not want a leader who would give up at the first disappointment. He wanted a leader who would battle on through adversity and go on leading his people in the good times and in the bad.

I am involved in training men and women for Christian ministry of various forms, and one of the things I emphasize is the need for courage and determination to go on serving God when it is rough as well as when it is easy. Those who do, make a significant contribution to the kingdom.

'Go, consecrate the people.'

The defeat at Ai was not caused by military weakness. It may have been caused by military over-confidence. But fundamentally the defeat at Ai was the consequence of sin, and therefore the people needed to be purified. I have noticed, both in my own life and in the life of those I counsel, that our power as individuals is related to the extent to which we seek God's purifying in our daily walk with him.

God was calling Joshua to holiness and purity. It was a call to be forgiven upon repentance. It is one thing to talk about being forgiven; it is another thing to go on living pure and holy lives. It is one thing to talk about being filled with the Spirit, it is another thing to go on walking with the Spirit day by day. Some start well and live bad. Others set off properly but become diverted down a whole range of cul-de-sacs which take their Christian lives nowhere. For Christians to have power in their lives they must first have purity.

Remember that purity is an essential requirement for power. Most Christians want power in their lives. They want to be able to heal the sick, to be able to witness with authority. But one of the keys to power is purity.

Verse 13 contains a call to holiness: 'Consecrate yourselves in preparation for tomorrow.' It does not seem long since the last time Joshua called on the people to do this: in Joshua 3:5 he told them: 'Consecrate yourselves for tomorrow the LORD will do amazing things among you.' In this previous instance they had to make themselves holy in order that the victory at Jericho would take place. In Joshua 7, they were to consecrate themselves so that the victory at Ai could take place. When they were fully consecrated, and the sin was exposed and dealt with, then victory would become possible. The key to victory in both Joshua 3 and in Joshua 7 is holiness, a complete submission to the living God.

Christians generally are much more at ease with being encouraged to be happy, than with being encouraged to be holy. Any message which involves having joy and blessing is easily received. But a sermon which calls for holiness is a different matter. I believe that the genuine seekers after God will be those who understand holiness as opposed to happiness.

Holiness and happiness are not always opposites. Sometimes we think that if we are holy we are bound to be miserable. But that is not true. Genuinely holy people are often very happy people. Why? Because they have submitted the self to the living God and they feel totally fulfilled. That is why being filled with the Holy Spirit is more than a matter of a fizz or a buzz or an emotional experience, important though that is; it is more than tongues or prophecy or healing power, important though they are. It is being filled with the Holy Spirit so that we can be consecrated to God.

Identifying the culprit

Before the promised victory, however, the sin must be dealt with:

'In the morning, present yourselves tribe by tribe. The tribe that the LORD takes shall come forward clan by clan; ... family by family; ... man by man. He who is caught with the devoted things shall be destroyed by fire, along with all that belongs to him. He has violated the covenant of the LORD and has done a disgraceful thing in Israel.'

The text at this point becomes quite frightening, as God homes in inexorably on the guilty person. The focus is on death and judgment.

In struggling to know how best to approach the passage, I came to the conclusion that I must simply allow its principles to speak for themselves. There is no getting away from the immense anger of the living God against rebellious individuals who choose to defy him.

Eventually a man called Achan was singled out. I am not sure how the process of identifying him took place: Joshua may have used the urim and the thummim, an Old Testament method similar to the casting of lots designed to determine God's will. At each stage, however, there would have been an opportunity for Achan to repent publicly. But he missed all the opportunities to respond.

Achan was singled out as the problem with the whole nation. Each of us needs to examine ourselves and ask whether our sinfulness is perhaps holding up the whole church family from moving forward. We do not need to become neurotic about it, we just need to make sure that we are in the right place with God, so that he will use the whole people of God.

The lust of the eyes

So the Israelites found out that Achan was the cause of the defeat (verse 19). His confession of his sin (verse 21) is a classic expression of 'the lust of the eyes': 'When I saw in the plunder a beautiful robe from Babylonia, two hundred shekels of silver and a wedge of gold weighing fifty shekels, I coveted them and took them': I saw, I coveted, and took. Saints of old used to describe the eyes as the windows of the soul. When we see things we tend to internalize them and the pressure of wanting them grows. If we had not seen them that pressure would not exist. The eyes are the source of an inappropriate or inordinate desire, which is the definition of lust. Although these are old-fashioned terms, the fact remains that lust was a problem two thousand years ago, and it is a problem now.

Lust operates on a number of levels. At a very simple level, the advertisements which bombard us in today's society, can, over a period of time, make us believe that we cannot exist without these products. So we buy into the lie of the materialistic society: we need these things if we are going to be the people we want to be. Most of the materialism in our society has been generated by what has been seen. The church has to reject the whole philosophy that *what we have* is more important than *who we are*.

It is vital that we do not buy into all the cultural surrounds of materialism, otherwise money that God needs for his purposes will be diverted from mission projects, from evangelism projects, from the social action projects. Achan had bought into the wrong value system. He thought, 'I want these things because it will be great for me, my wife and family.' But they were evidences of a corrupt civilization. God wanted the children of Israel to have nothing to do with them, in order that they could be pure and holy and right with him.

Materialism is not the only way that the lust of the eyes affects believers. Many Christian men, after seeing a woman dressed in a particular way, or watching a sexually explicit video, allow what they see to be interpreted sexually in their minds. They betray what God has called them to be as pure followers of Jesus. Men must guard their eyes if they are to be pure in a world where sexual immorality is rampant.

For both men and women, the lusts of the eyes cause jealousy as they see others being honoured or blessed in some way. The little green idol of envy rises within because of what the eyes have seen. 'Watch your eyes' is the message from the sin of Achan.

Achan died because of his sin. When we covet illegitimate things, however attractive they may appear, it results in our spiritual death. There are Christians with whom everything seems all right on the surface, but because they have gone after something that God did not want them to have, their inner spiritual life has been stifled. God sorrows, because he wants to have our best, and instead he sees his children suffering and dying spiritually. The moment of passing happiness is as nothing compared with what they are laying up for the future.

'Over Achan they heaped up a large pile of rocks, which remains to this day' (7:26). The heap of rocks was to be a type of visual aid for the children of Israel. Like you and I, they had very short memories. God wanted them to remember what had happened to Achan.

10

Leading a restored people
Joshua 8:1-29

The Israelites experience an incredible jump from being broken and defeated and despairing, to being a conquering army again. They had the mountain-top experience of Jericho, followed by the valley-experience of the sin of Achan, returning eventually to another mountain-top experience at Ai.

Now that Achan's sin had been dealt with, the Israelites move on to conquer Ai. They had no choice really: they could not go back because there was nothing for them in the wilderness, and they could not conquer the land of Canaan without defeating the people of Ai. Ai and other mountain towns were strategic military outposts that guarded the plains beyond, down towards the Mediterranean. God told Joshua that this time he was to take the whole army with him. We may be forgiven for imagining a touch of humour in God's voice here, because when they last went up to Ai they only sent a few men. The word 'Ai' means 'ruin' or 'sacked city'. 'Go up to the ruin and make it a ruin' is the Hebrew meaning here.

'You shall do to Ai and its king as you did to Jericho and its king, except that you may carry off their plunder and livestock for yourselves' (8:2). What an incredible irony that is! One chapter earlier Achan cannot contain his greed and takes what is not his. If only he had waited! If only he had had the patience to wait for God's timing, he would have shared in the tremendous blessing God had for everybody. But no, he wanted it in his time and in his way.

What a word for us today! Impatience is ungodly. The desire for instant gratification is a distinctive feature of modern society. Its influence can hinder us greatly in our walk with God. Many of us want to run ahead of God. And when God does not seem to provide what we want, we make our own arrangements. We provide it for ourselves by human stealth or ingenuity.

Jericho was like the firstfruits, like the tithe in the Old Testament. Give to God his share and the rest was for your own use.

Dealing with discouragement

After the first defeat at Ai because of Achan's sin, Joshua's standing with the people of God was probably not very high. He may have felt discouraged as a leader. And probably the people of God were feeling discouraged too. So it is likely there was general desperation and a loss of nerve in the camp.

Today, the church of Jesus, locally and nationally, can so easily lose its nerve. We are surrounded by thousands of people who do not know Jesus, and we can be overwhelmed by a culture that is largely secular. We ask, 'Are we ever going to see this world won for our Lord Jesus?' Discouragement comes even upon those who have vision and passion to see God's kingdom come in power.

This chapter calls us not to lose our nerve. Who will speak to the nation? Not the politicians. Not a despondent crowd of defeated Christians afraid of being in a minority! But Christians are God's chosen instruments and though we are small in number, the gates of Hell will not prevail against us.

God looks for faithfulness and commitment from us, and will grant the victory even in situations where we are despondent.

The Lord said to Joshua, 'Do not be afraid, and do not be discouraged' (8:1). Notice that the 'Do not be afraid' and 'Do not be discouraged' do not mean that Joshua abdicates all responsibility for the enterprise. When God says, 'Do not be afraid', he requires the combination of two things in order to see victory: divine initiative and human co-operation.

For some reason God chooses to use people to fulfil his purposes. He was not going to take Ai for the people of Israel. He gave them a strategy, but he will not do it for them; he will do it with them. God will not win your community to Christ *for* you, he will win the community to Christ *with* you. Remember always that the divine and the human element must come together. We have to learn to be the answers to our own prayers by co-operating with the divine.

Joshua would never have seen Ai defeated unless he had stepped out in faith with God. Even the miraculous depends on us taking the step of faith. Remember when Israel was standing on the edge of the Jordan. When did the water part? When their feet touched the water, not before. We have to take a step of faith to see the miracle, not wait for the miracle before we take the step of faith.

There is victory promised in the Christian life. Joshua went to Ai with confidence that God would be with him and that ultimate victory would be his. We have failures, we make mistakes and we suffer defeats, but ultimately, we know that there is a destiny for all who believe, which is total victory, either when Jesus returns to earth to claim his people, or we die. But whichever of those happens first, the ultimate victory is assured.

So Joshua and the whole army moved out to attack Ai. They did what God had told them to do. The key phrase is at the end of verse 8: 'Do what the LORD has commanded. See to it; you have my orders.'

God's mouthpiece

In a way, Joshua's words 'You have my orders' are a bit presumptuous. After all, they were not really his orders at all; they were God's orders. But this situation helps us to understand the nature of true leadership, whatever area it relates to. The nature of true Christian leadership is that we speak the words of God. If we are to be leaders whom God can use, then we have to be those who are the mouthpiece of God.

If you are leading other people in a Christian service of any kind, then your leadership is valid only insofar as it reflects what God wants to happen in the situation. We are not leaders by virtue of personality, or intellect, or confidence. We are leaders by virtue of gifting, and our leadership is authenticated in as far as we mouth God's words after him.

If at any point in our leading we drift from what God says, our ministry ceases to be distinguished by the mark of integrity God desires. Today's churches need the kind of leadership they have lacked for much of this century. They need people in leadership positions who hear from God and tell us what he says. They need strong and visionary leadership. They do not need the leadership of the bureaucrat or the functionary or the time-serving official.

Leaders are not called to worry about what God says. True, everything must be checked out against Scripture and with other leaders and mature Christians to be sure that God has been heard correctly. But once he has been heard, the leaders' task is not to negotiate away God's claims, but to be obedient. The children of Israel took Ai because they did what God said. They followed the strategy of Joshua which was revealed to him by God.

There are occasions when a debate is unhelpful. The influence of our culture, which challenges and questions authority at every level, has so affected Christians that we even question God's authority to run his church his way. Joshua and the Israelites would never have captured Ai if they had not been fully convinced that God's word for them was the only thing that really mattered.

At the end of the day, we need to ask this question: Whose church is it anyway? The answer is not the elders' or other leaders', or any other sort of grouping. Ultimately, it is God's church. In other words, Jesus is the head of the body and all believers, including leaders, are members of the body. God is in control. We are not in a negotiating position with him. It is our place to be obedient to the King.

11

Taking stock
Joshua 8:30-35

After Ai had been destroyed and the king defeated, there seems to be a pause in the campaign to conquer Canaan as the Israelites gather at Mount Ebal to renew their covenant with God. It is peculiar that there should have been a pause here. One would think that Joshua, having conquered Jericho and Ai, would continue to push on and take as much of the land as he could.

The whole group, having conquered Ai, made a journey thirty miles north to an area that was in the middle of the land God had given them. The journey may have taken a few days, before they stood, half of them before Mount Ebal, and half before Mount Gerizim. There they renewed their covenant and their vow with God. They realized they could not continue without taking stock.

We in the church in Britain today have much to learn from this. We should be taking stock regularly if we want to be the kind of church where people will come and hear God's Word proclaimed, be blessed by its teaching, and transformed by an encounter with God. The same applies to us as individuals. We should be taking stock of our own lives, finding out what God is saying to us about our walk with him.

The Israelites, by this act, were fulfilling a commitment made to Moses many years earlier, when he gave instructions to bless the people of Israel when they had taken the Promised Land. When they were all assembled 'Joshua read all the

In the presence of the Israelites, Joshua copied on stones the law of Moses which Moses had written (8:32). This would be on a fairly large stone, probably six feet or more in height, and Joshua would chisel on to these stones the law of Moses. I doubt that he copied the entire law of Moses because it would take a long time. Personally, I think he chiselled the Ten Commandments.

However, in Iran, archaeologists have discovered an obelisk, about eight feet high, on which there is chiselled in very small lettering a statement that is three times the length of the Book of Deuteronomy. So it could have been a very substantial piece of work that Joshua wrote.

It is thought that he chiselled it by using a type of wet cement which when it dried hardened into the surface of the stone. Or it could be the ancient practice of using a kind of dye to make markings on the stone.

The aliens (8:33, 35) were those who became attached to the children of Israel as they wandered through the wilderness. As they journeyed, nomadic peoples joined them, possibly for protection. Most of these aliens would have sat loose to the structure of the Israelite tribes; yet they would still be welcomed because God had been quite clear that just because someone was not an Israelite, did not mean that they were to be rejected out of hand.

words of the law – the blessings and the curses – just as it is written in the Book of the Law. There was not a word of all that Moses had commanded that Joshua did not read to the whole assembly of Israel' (8:34-35).

Why do they focus on Moses' law? Because they were taking stock of what had been given to them by God in his covenant with them.

Now a covenant is where two parties make a contract to abide by a certain set of rules and values, and to be in a relationship with one another. That is what God had done with the people of Israel. They were in relationship with each other. He gave them a series of laws and rules they needed to follow in order to show they were his people. If they fulfilled their side of the covenant then there would be divine blessing; but if they failed to keep God's commands, the blessing would be withheld.

Now that seems to me to be a very powerful emphasis for us as believers today. We too are in a covenant relationship with God, with a whole range of commitments. As time goes by, we start to dishonour those commitments. We need to say to God, 'I have failed to honour those commitments, I am sorry. I ask to be forgiven. Please help me make a fresh start.'

We are also in covenant with other members of the church because as Christians we are members of God's family. This means that every time we do anything that destroys that partnership and covenant, by gossiping or backbiting or greed or in any other way, we are in breech of a very serious covenant. God says to each of us today: 'Have you damaged a relationship within the body? Have you hurt a fellow believer?'

There is also the covenant of marriage. Some of us fail to

fulfil that precious covenant by our behaviour, our actions and our attitudes. We need forgiveness for such behaviour. Marital breakdown is not the work of a moment, but is caused by individual betrayals taking place over a long period of time, undermining the covenant. God says to those who are married: 'Is your covenantal relationship right with your marriage partner?'

God wants us to take stock. That is the whole thrust of this passage. Take time out to look at the Book of the Law, to study the Scripture and give to God, not only financially, but with time and energy and effort.

Some people may find that in order to take stock they need to set aside a whole day. Personally, I find it very helpful on a regular basis to go through the principles of church membership; at other times I reflect on basic principles of discipleship in the Bible. I ask myself: Where am I with regard to those simple commitments? Where am I giving myself? Where am I in respect to witnessing to my faith? Where am I in reading my Bible and praying? Where am I in being open to the power of the Holy Spirit? And so on.

The principles are so simple, but we often take them for granted, and we rush on. That is great if the ground on which we are rushing has a good foundation. But many of us have not got the foundation right and are building on sand. The first time there is a storm our work collapses in a heap and we wonder why.

Heed the warnings as well as the blessings
Joshua did not just read the good bits of the law! We read in 8:35, 'Joshua read all the words of the law – the blessings as well as the curses'. Do you have some favourite bits of the

Bible you return to again and again? There is nothing wrong with that. But the danger is that we develop a 'favourite verse mentality' to Scripture, taking only the teachings we like and ignoring those teachings we do not like. Denominations do that all the time. Emphasizing what seems to support them and shying away from what does not. When we treat the Bible in this way we are sitting in judgment on Scripture. We want to let our personality and background dictate to the Bible, whereas it is supposed to be the other way round. We are supposed to read the blessings and the curses, the bits we like and the bits we do not like.

How we need to take that word to heart! If we do not we will be off balance as individuals and as a church. There are too many 'single-issue fanatics' in the life of the church. These people take a thoroughly biblical idea – social action, worship, evangelism, Bible study or whatever – and go for it so strongly that they are negative about anything else. It really is a sign of immaturity. The mature Christian, however, is someone who is passionately committed to the whole counsel of God.

12

Danger of deception
Joshua 9:1-27

The inhabitants of the Promised Land were terrified by the immense power and success of the Israelites. Therefore the kings towards the Mediterranean Sea decided that an alliance of force was the only way to stop Israel. They probably had not been together for a long time due to inter-tribal warfare, but, confronted by the might of the Israelites, they joined forces to stop this massive threat which faced them. The Gibeonites, however, decided to approach the matter differently. They realized they were not strong enough to defeat Israel, so they decided to try to trick Joshua and the leaders to make a peace pact with them.

The possibility of deception

> The people of Gibeon ... resorted to a ruse: They went as a delegation whose donkeys were loaded with worn-out sacks.... The men put worn and parched sandals on their feet and wore old clothes. All the bread of their food supply was dry and mouldy. Then they went to Joshua.... 'We have come from a distant country; make a treaty with us' (9:4-6).

Israel had just renewed their covenant with God (Joshua 8). Yet immediately after this act of commitment, they were deceived by the Gibeonites. This is a reminder that when we are most spiritually in tune with God, at our most committed to him, we are also vulnerable to deception.

106

The children of Israel were marching on to victory. Soon they would take over the whole land. But they were deceived by pieces of mouldy bread. How easy it is to be deceived!

There are many men and women who once walked with God, who served and followed him, some were preachers of the gospel, whose lives have descended into total spiritual disintegration because they were deceived by the evil one. Those deceptions can occur morally, theologically or relationally.

If your pastor were to ask you: 'Would you commit adultery, or would you be involved in a relationship that involved fornication?' you would likely say, 'No.' But for many, the subtle betrayal that began the deception was the slightly dodgy friendship that was allowed to continue. Perhaps it was coloured with spirituality: 'We pray together', but they deluded themselves into believing that they were doing right. I have heard people who supposedly love the Lord Jesus defend the most outrageous immoral sin, on the grounds that God has told them it is all right. How did they get to that stage? Because they were deceived by the evil one.

Others are deceived theologically. They drift into a nominal commitment. The sects actually see the church as one of the most fertile recruiting grounds for their particular operation. They know that there is an openness to religious faith on the fringes of the church; they look for people who do not really know what they believe and are quite open to being drawn away.

Moral deception usually results in a person leaving the church and losing any semblance of real faith. *Theological* deception usually leads to a person moving away from the mainstream of Christianity into a cult or extremist religious group. But *relational* deception is, in some ways, more dangerous still, because people who fall prey to this form of deception usually stay within the church of Jesus. Relational deception occurs when individuals arrogantly believe that they are right and everybody else is wrong. Judgmentalism runs and ruins their life. They have been deceived into believing the supremacy of their own opinions on every subject. That is a delusion.

Believers are always in danger of being deceived.

The road to deception

The Gibeonites appealed to the Israelites' *pride*. Firstly they said: 'We are your servants' (9:8). They placed themselves under the authority of Joshua, and the leaders felt good about themselves. Secondly the Gibeonites said: 'You have a great God' (9:9-10). Pride is the classic way for deception to come into the church, into a Christian community and into individuals.

The Israelites, like us, would recognize how wrong it was to cave in to a threat. But the appeal to our vanity can be a much more potent weapon than a threat to our safety. Few of us can resist the appeal to our vanity.

So, through flattery, the Israelites made a basic mistake: 'The men of Israel sampled their provisions but did not inquire of the LORD' (9:14).

They were right to check the state of the Gibeonites' provisions. In combating deception we must use our minds to analyse what is right and wrong. Common sense does not disappear out of the window when Christianity comes in. However, they needed the dimension of the Spirit, too. They should have enquired of the Lord, but they did not. Enquiring of the Lord is the great protection against deception. It is really important.

To enquire of the Lord means to listen to him. There are many groups, established in churches nationwide, which believe themselves to be incredibly holy and spiritual. But they are asking God to baptise their prejudices and work them out: 'Dear God, you know we need this in our church, do this. You know we need that in our denomination: do that. You know we need this in our house group: do this.' But they are not enquiring of the Lord, they are telling the Lord. This leads nowhere. Christians need to be careful that they actually ask God what he approves.

The Israelites, however, having forgotten to ask God whether their action was right, 'made a treaty of peace with them to let them live, and the leaders of the assembly ratified it by oath' (9:15).

The result of deception

'Three days after they made the treaty with the Gibeonites, the Israelites heard that they were neighbours living near them' (9:16). As the Israelites had made a vow to protect these people, they could not take revenge on them for their deception. So they settled for making them into slaves for the Israelite community.

Often those who are in the sad state of having gone down the morally deceived route of a sinful relationship, try to pretend on the surface that everything is fine. But the bondage in which they find themselves is obvious.

It is similar for those who have gone down the road of theological deception, ending up far away from where the Lord wants them to be. There can be superficial signs of happiness and joy, but deeper within there is bondage.

Often I have been told that Christianity is narrow,

constricting and binding; all those rules and regulations! It is constricting to say one must drive on the left-hand side of the road only and not on the right. But it happens to be the safest way. It is narrow in its definition, but it preserves life and provides protection. Freedom to do your own thing theologically, or morally, or relationally, only leads to bondage. People who fall for the lie become increasingly wrapped up in themselves and their own sinfulness. A man wrapped up in himself is a very small package.

And this really is the thrust of chapter 9. The Gibeonites become slaves because of their attempt to deceive, and in that sense, they were punished. The children of Israel, for their part, found themselves with a whole nation to both subdue and protect, because they allowed themselves to be deceived.

How to avoid deception

Firstly, the key to avoiding deception is *humility*. We have already seen the appeal to pride in verses 7-15. The men and women who will not be deceived morally, theologically or relationally are those who are humble. I worry so much when I hear Christians contemptuously dismissing other believers, be they church leaders or lay people. Humility is crucial. If Joshua and the people had not been so swelled from recent victories, there would have been a far less chance of their being conned by such flattering behaviour. But pride was their downfall.

Secondly, believers need to be marked by *prayerfulness*. The Israelites did not enquire of the Lord. If we want to avoid deception in what God is saying in our church life or to us individually, we must *pray*. Otherwise we may be wise with our minds yet miss out on the divine dimension.

Thirdly, we must have *right relationships with our leaders*. In verse 18 the writer says this: 'The whole assembly grumbled against the leaders.' How relevant this is! Government-baiting, for example, seems to be the sport of the moment. Right across the board everybody moans about their leaders.

As long as you stay out of leadership you will be relatively safe from criticism. But as soon as you move into some kind of leadership it is those you are leading who are likely to grumble at your leadership. Once you establish some kind of leadership role, there are those who will want to object to the way you are doing it. That is the nature of humanity and we live with that.

A right relationship with their leader would have helped the children of Israel all through the desert wanderings. But they moaned continually at Moses. Joshua found out that they did not always treat him any better. When a group of believers get out of right relationship with their leadership, there will be a tendency to shoot off at an angle from the mainstream of what God is wanting. It is deluding to believe that you are right and the leaders are wrong.

As believers we are in enemy territory; therefore we are in danger of being deceived. On one occasion, before travelling abroad, I was given four injections. I was about to go to a territory where I needed protection and immunization from dangers. Christians are in enemy territory and we need immunization against the devil's attack. It is largely the powerful, living Word of God which protects us from deceit. Take it; it is medication which works and which will last all our lives. But we also need humility, prayerfulness and right relationships to keep us on God's straight and narrow path.

13

On the victory side
Joshua 10:1-15

Adonizedek, the king of Jerusalem was afraid. In a crescent to the north of Jerusalem were Jericho, Ai and Gibeon. Jericho and Ai were destroyed and Gibeon had become vassals of Israel. He could see his territory being increasingly encroached on by the invading army to which he was now exposed. His own situation was becoming increasingly vulnerable.

Therefore he decided to take revenge on Gibeon for making a treaty with the Israelites. He was not willing to do so with his own army alone, so he asked four neighbouring kings to help him punish the Gibeonites.

When the five kings of the Amorites attacked the city of Gibeon, the Gibeonites sent word to Joshua at Gilgal to come and help. Joshua marched to Gibeon with his entire army, assured by God of complete victory. The Hittites fled before Israel, and as they fled the Lord hurled huge hailstones down upon them from the sky. More were killed by the hailstones than by the Israelites. Joshua asked the Lord for the sun and moon to stand still until Israel's enemies were destroyed.

This incident brings to light some significant principles about battle and warfare. They were true for Joshua and, I believe, they are true for us today in the spiritual warfare in which all Christians are engaged.

Three strategies for victory

Notice, in verse 6, that the Gibeonites sent word to Joshua: 'Do not abandon your servants.' As we saw in the last chapter, the Israelites had been duped into a treaty with the Gibeonites that they now had to honour. Having made a promise, Joshua acts in integrity. Joshua could have seen this situation as a way to get rid of the Gibeonites who had conned him into making a wrong decision. But he did the right thing. This, then is the first strategy for overcoming our enemies: a requirement in spiritual warfare is *to do the right thing*.

Now some may think: 'Well, that's obvious.' But it is not always obvious when we come under pressure. When we are under pressure in a spiritual warfare situation, the tendency is to compromise and to go for the easiest way out, rather than to do what is right.

Doing the right thing is very 'anti' the spirit of the day. The popular mood is expediency, pragmatism. In the sixties this came to be known as 'situational ethics'. In other words, what is right is determined by the context of the situation. Do not worry too much about absolute rights and wrongs; do what feels good now in this particular situation.

Many Christians, leaders included, would have been preserved and protected from falling in the spiritual battle, if they had done what was right rather than what they felt like doing.

I see a parade of people in the church nationwide who are casualties of spiritual warfare, because this single principle has been ignored. At the beginning of the temptation, they knew the right thing to do, but they settled instead for the easier route of compromise.

If you are facing a massive temptation to compromise in

your life, the key to spiritual victory is firstly to do what is right, as set out in God's Word, however costly. When you do what is right, God honours your commitment to integrity and will rescue you in the spiritual battle. Too many people, because they give in at stage one, are compromised; and because they are, future victories are very difficult.

The second strategy for victory is unity. Christians are strengthened when they *act together*. Joshua took with him his entire army including all the best fighting men (9:7). There was strength as the people of God acted together. In the battle against the world, the flesh and the devil, and the ordinary human dilemmas that face us all, we are strengthened when we operate together in fellowship with the body of Christ.

Being Christian lone-rangers is a very dangerous position. We are always more likely to be protected when we function within the body of Christ. That is why being part of a church family is so crucial in the fight against temptation. We must have those with whom we can share our struggles. Be it a big church or a small church, be it a house group, a special prayer group, or a special friend, it does not really matter as long as it is an expression of the corporate activity of the body of Christ.

Together we are strong; divided we are easy prey for Satan to pick off and destroy. The stragglers, those who push on ahead faster than everybody else, those who go off at a tangent, all these are in danger of being picked off by the evil one.

Many heresies in church history have been started by individuals who have gone off and done their own thing, refusing to be under anybody else's authority, refusing to consult in any meaningful way. They have gathered around themselves like-minded men and women who refuse to challenge their basic presuppositions, and so become isolated, surrounded merely by yes-men.

How are believers going to defeat Satan, the world and the flesh? By a commitment to integrity whatever the cost and a commitment to operating together as the people of God.

The third principle is *divine intervention*, the promise of support from the King of kings, the ultimate Warrior Commander and Lord of lords. Without that promise we cannot succeed even if the other two principles are in place.

Joshua's great success as a military strategist was not simply that he was an ancient General Montgomery. He certainly was a skilled strategist. But he won because he had tapped into a divine authority.

The bottom line is that all these enemy forces – the world, the flesh and the devil – bow to the authority of Jesus Christ. That is why we need to be tapping daily into the resources of the divine. We are engaged in warfare that humanly speaking we cannot win. But Jesus has already, by his death and resurrection, defeated the powers of darkness. Satan has been mortally wounded, and our sinful nature was given an incredible blow when the Holy Spirit came to live inside us.

The victory has been won in Christ and we are to receive it by God's power. Day by day we need to be drawing on those sources. Just as he helped Joshua, so he longs to help us in the temptations and struggles and battles that we face. On the days when we feel frustrated and angry at the lack of progress; on the days when we will feel incredibly defeated because plans and prayers and the work of months seem to have come to nothing; on the days when personal relationships foul up for almost no reason, we will need God's power. Without it we will be overwhelmed by the forces around us.

14

Darkness before the dawn
Joshua 10:16-11:23

Why all the violence?

In the passage from Joshua 10:16-11:23 we find the most concentrated amount of bloodshed, death, destruction and warfare in the entire book. The Old Testament does deal with violence and death in a way that most of us at the end of the twentieth century find abhorrent, so it is important to understand why God commanded Joshua to kill all these people.

It will not be easy, but it will be an opportunity to engage our minds with some difficult material from God's Word. Hopefully it will strengthen our faith and call us to a new level of commitment and holiness in our walk with God.

Look at the following verses from the Book of Joshua in which such activity is described.

When the trumpets sounded the people shouted and at the sound of the trumpet, when the people gave a loud shout, the wall collapsed. So every man charged straight in and they took the city. They devoted the city to the LORD and destroyed with the sword every living thing in it: men and women, young and old, cattle, sheep and donkeys (Joshua 6:20-21).

Then Joshua, together with all Israel, took Achan, son of Zerah, the silver, the robe, the gold wedge, his sons and daughters, his cattle, donkeys and sheep, his tent and all that he had, to the Valley of Achor. Joshua said: 'Why have you brought this disaster on us? The LORD will bring disaster on you today.' Then all Israel stoned him and after they had stoned the rest they burned them (Joshua 7:24-25).

The men of the ambush also came out of the city against them, so that they were caught in the middle, with Israelites on both sides. Israel cut them down, leaving them neither survivors nor fugitives, but they took the king of Ai alive and brought him to Joshua.

When Israel had finished killing all the men of Ai in the fields and in the desert where they had chased them, and when every one of them had been put to the sword, all the Israelites returned to Ai and killed those who were in it. Twelve thousand men and women fell that day – all the people of Ai (Joshua 8:22-25).

The dilemma is not the warfare itself, for modern warfare has seen millions more killed than there were in Old Testament times. Mankind has always been at war. The dilemma is that God seems to be telling Joshua to butcher all these men, women and children. Over the years I have grappled with this issue. Is the God of Joshua the same God who is revealed in Jesus in the New Testament?

Principles of interpretation

There are six principles we need to bear in mind when we are interpreting the Old Testament in general, and Joshua in particular!

1. *The Old Testament is on the dark side of the cross*. What do I mean by that? There is unquestionably a clarity of revelation after the cross which we do not find before it. Much of the teaching of the Bible is clearer in light of the death of Jesus than it was before it. So it is important that we do not pretend that the New Testament is the same as the Old or *vice versa*.

Old Testament believers were not Christians in the sense that we understand the term. That does not mean they were not right with God. But they did not know of the death and resurrection of Jesus. Even the prophets who had a vague awareness that a Messiah was coming did not know the details.

Reading Old Testament passages is like being in a room with a candle in the corner. The room is mainly shadow. It is not until the bright light of Jesus dawns that everything becomes clear.

2. *We should always interpret the unclear in the light of the clear, not the other way round*. In other words, we must not come to these passages in Joshua and say, 'What kind of God have we got here who destroys all these people?', and then forget all the teaching of the New Testament which seems to be contrary to it. We have to interpret what we read in Joshua in the light of the clarity of the New Testament. We must not read Joshua in isolation and claim it describes a God who does this kind of thing, and then worry about the fact that all the New Testament must therefore be untrue.

3. *We have to affirm that the Bible is true*. Now that is obvious. But to grapple with the Bible is to grapple with a very difficult book, sixty-six books, in fact, written by about

forty authors over approximately 2,000 years. It is written in three languages: Hebrew, Greek and Aramaic. Parts of the Bible can be a struggle to work out at times, but it is all still true. We are not to play about with the truthfulness of Scripture, but to try and understand what it means.

4. *In the Bible there are different kinds of literature.* When it says in Scripture that the trees of the field shall clap their hands, I do not believe that the trees are all going to grow literal hands and start clapping them. But I am not in any sense compromising my commitment to the integrity of the Word of God.

Different kinds of literature are meant to be read in different ways. The Book of Joshua is a different kind of literature to the Book of Romans or the Book of Revelation for that matter. Joshua is an historical account of a people conquering a land. It is given to show God's dealing with his people. The Book of Romans, on the other hand, is a letter from the apostle Paul, in which he writes about Christian doctrine and behaviour. The difference is similar to that between a book about the Norman Conquest on the one hand, and a car manual on the other. So Joshua is not the same thing as a New Testament teaching book and must not be read in the same way.

5. *Human understanding of God develops.* In the Bible the understanding of the way God operates does not remain static. Take, for example, the doctrine of resurrection. Early saints such as Abraham, Isaac, Jacob and Moses had a very limited understanding of what resurrection meant; but as we move on to the prophets we see they had a better understanding. When

you get to Jesus he is actually resurrected and in the light of that, Paul's doctrine of the resurrection is crystal clear. So there is a sense of progression.

Even as Christians, our understanding of God develops. When we are first converted we have a very limited view of God. As we mature, our view of God changes. One of the signs of immaturity is that we try to make God do what we want him to. As we develop in maturity, we learn that despite what we want, God does have standards and values and he acts in a particular way.

6. *We need to beware twentieth century arrogance*. We must not read the Book of Joshua thinking that what modern people believe must be right and all the other previous generations have got it wrong. We live in a sick and twisted culture. Along with other cultures down the ages we have a great deal to apologise for. Any culture which can produce butter, wine and meat mountains, while thousands starve; that can see the tribal hatred in Ruanda without taking drastic action to curb it surely has no right to claim arrogantly that we have got it all right and the people of the Old Testament were just poor primitives.

These six principles help us to understand the Book of Joshua.

Moving on from this there are some further general points about the invasion of Canaan of which we need to be aware.

1. *The Canaanites were totally depraved*. The evidence is that the Canaanite culture was depraved in a way that was almost unknown in the ancient world. Their worship of gods was grotesque. It involved a whole range of bestial activities.

There was cult prostitution, both heterosexual and homo-sexual. They offered child sacrifices, which involved boys as young as eight being thrown alive into a red hot furnace. Women were sexually and physically abused. Children had their bones broken at random in order to suppress the wrath of the gods. The list just goes on and on. Canaanite society was evil and totally depraved. Joshua was not dealing with a few peasant farmers.

2. *Canaanite practice was occultic*. Objects were invested and endued with power. Today the occult is sensationalized in films and TV programmes. But genuine occult practice is sinister and frightening in the horrible, powerful grip it has on people's lives. Certain objects were endued with demonic

---

We should not confuse the teaching of Jesus in the New Testament on personal behaviour, with the Old Testament teaching about the behaviour of the state. When Jesus said his disciples should forgive seventy times seven, that was not a contradiction of criminals being put to death. They are two different issues. The death penalty is related to the way a state operates; the teaching of Jesus is concerned with the way individuals relate to each other.

If you kill a man's wife, he has no right to kill you in revenge. But the state may choose to take your life after a legal procedure, or it may choose to incarcerate you for the rest of your natural life. Christians are divided on the question of capital punishment but one cannot simply quote words of Jesus to justify the abolition of the death penalty.

power and Satan used them to bring death, disease and
destruction into people's lives. That is why objects such as
tents, clothing and animals were destroyed by Joshua. Many
of them were associated with occult practices and God did
not want the people of Israel to be contaminated by anything
evil.

3. *The killings were merciful.* I am using 'merciful' in the
Old Testament situation, not in the context of today. The vast
majority of marauding armies in Old Testament times did not
simply kill people; rape and torture were the order of the
day. What happened in the Book of Joshua was a straightforward strike through a nation, in a clear military fashion,
putting everyone to the sword. Whatever the Israelites did
was merciful when compared to the actions of other nations
at the same time.

God's ultimate Word

If you had been with Joshua when God was commanding him
to do these things, I doubt whether you would have heard
anything. It was Joshua's internal conviction. These events
occurred on what we have called the dark side of the cross,
and it is my view that Joshua correctly understood what God
wanted in terms of principle, but sometimes wrongly in terms
of practice. When I say wrongly, I mean simply that Joshua
was a victim of the culture of his day. What we have in these
Old Testament passages is not prescriptive, but descriptive.

I am sure that God wanted sin punished; I am sure that
God wanted evil practices stamped out; I am sure that God
wanted his holy reign and rule to be put in place. But it was
interpreted through the culture of the day, just as we also

interpret God's Word through the culture of our day.

And as progressive revelation developed through Scripture, the people understood more and more of what God really wanted, rather than drawing on their own cultural expectations. By the time we get to Jesus, all the cultural fog has been blown away and we see clearly because the final revelation, God's ultimate word in Christ, has been revealed.

Therefore I believe the God of Joshua is the God of Paul. He is the same God who is consistently working out his purposes in history. But human beings did not hear him clearly until the final revelation in Christ, because they lived in the darkness before the coming of God's holy Son.

The problem of Achan's children

All this, however, still leaves the question of why Achan and his children had to be killed. There are two issues here: firstly, the severity of the punishment and, secondly, the involvement of Achan's family in the punishment.

With regard to the first point, the offence had to be punished by death to avert *the danger of corruption*. If Achan had not been punished severely, it is likely that his insidious, sinful influence would have affected all the children of Israel. The whole purpose of invading the land to provide a place for the people of God would have been destroyed from the beginning.

The second issue is rather more complex: Why did Achan's children have to die? Deuteronomy 24:16 says this: 'Fathers shall not be put to death for their children, nor children put to death for their fathers; each is to die for his own sin.' Joshua would have been aware of this teaching, so we are left with a choice: either Joshua did the wrong thing and should not have had Achan's children killed, or the children were willing accomplices. We do not read anything about babies in this passage, so these may well have been grown-up children. Perhaps the children were willing accomplices and were just as guilty as Achan was. Death, therefore, would have been the fitting punishment.

15

Issues of victory
Joshua 12-21

Chapter 12 records the names of the thirty-one kings defeated by Joshua and his warring people. The chapter is a review of all that God had done to bring victory.

Chapter 13 through to chapter 21 deals with the allocation of the territory that had been taken. In chapter 13, there is the remaining land still to be taken. Chapters 14 and 15 describe the division of land to the west of Jordan between the tribes of Reuben, Gad and Manasseh. Chapters 16-21 deal with the allocations for the remaining tribes.

In addition to this factual narrative, in these chapters there are four significant points that I would like to highlight.

The first point to note is found in 13:1: 'When Joshua was old and well advanced in years, the LORD said to him, "You are very old, and there are still very large areas of land to be taken over."' We cannot be sure how old Joshua was at this point, possibly still in his eighties. The implication is that he is to make a list of the land yet to be conquered so that other leaders could take over the task. Interestingly, Joshua was given his own town to settle down in. Knowing Joshua he probably did not have too much of a retirement; people would have asked him for advice and he would continue to think about God's plan and purposes. But from this point onwards his role is no longer central.

This is a reminder to us that *the task of God is always greater than an individual in the purposes of God*. However

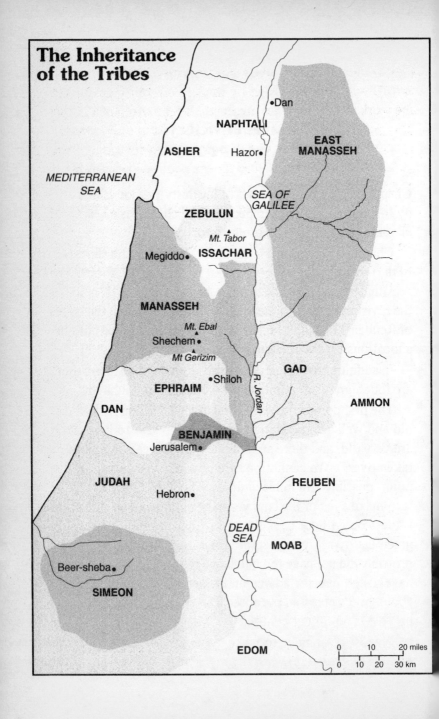

The Inheritance of the Tribes

•Dan

NAPHTALI

ASHER

Hazor•

EAST MANASSEH

MEDITERRANEAN SEA

SEA OF GALILEE

ZEBULUN

▲ *Mt. Tabor*

Megiddo•

ISSACHAR

MANASSEH

▲ *Mt. Ebal*

Shechem•

▲ *Mt Gerizim*

•Shiloh

GAD

EPHRAIM

R. Jordan

DAN

AMMON

BENJAMIN

Jerusalem•

JUDAH

Hebron•

REUBEN

DEAD SEA

MOAB

Beer-sheba•

SIMEON

EDOM

| 0 | 10 | 20 miles |
| 0 | 10 | 20 | 30 km |

long we have been involved, we will come inevitably to the point when we leave either by moving out or by death. Yet the work in which we are involved must be continued by the next generation. That is why it is absurd for the advanced in years to hold on to things when they ought to be passing them on to others. It is also absurd for the young to be dismissive of the work which has gone before them.

Previous believers formed the foundation for all that we enjoy today. And we, by our prayer and faithfulness, will perform a foundation service for those who follow after us. Your particular ministry is only part of the great scheme of ministry that God has had before us and will have after us.

Joshua was ready now to pass on the baton to another relay runner who would pick it up and run the next leg. We should be looking over our shoulders, saying: 'How can I prepare those who follow me to pick up the baton and run on the race firmly with the living God?'

We come to the second significant point in Joshua 14:6-14. Here we read about Caleb, Joshua's fellow spy from years past, and now also old:

> Now the men of Judah approached Joshua at Gilgal, and Caleb the son of Jephunneh the Kenezite said to him, 'You know what the LORD said to Moses ... about you and me. I was forty years old when Moses the servant of the LORD sent me to Kadesh Barnea to explore the land ... I, however, followed the LORD my God wholeheartedly. So on that day Moses swore to me, "The land on which your feet have walked will be your inheritance and that of your children for ever, because you have followed the LORD my God wholeheartedly"' (14:6-7, 9).

The second point is this: *be faithful*. Caleb was forty years old when Moses sent him to explore the land; he was faithful to God and was known as someone who followed the Lord wholeheartedly (verse 9). Moses had promised Caleb that the land on which his feet had walked would be his inheritance (Deuteronomy 1:36).

Caleb wanted what was promised him forty-five years previously! What a memory! Caleb had spent forty-five years waiting for this promise to be fulfilled. Why was he getting it? Because he was a faithful man. The key to his success was that he was 'wholehearted'.

The Bible is full of commendations, particularly in the Old Testament, for those who do not serve God with partial hearts. The psalmist prayed that God would give him an undivided heart (Psalm 86:11). A divided heart is one where the will, the emotions and the mind are given over to one thing but a bit is left for something else. In other words, the psalmist wanted to be wholehearted in his commitment. And Caleb was a man wholeheartedly given to God.

Today there is so much pressure to serve God with a divided heart. In terms of our money, time and energy, it is very easy to be half-hearted in our Christian service. By half-hearted I do not mean casual; I mean that something else creeps in and dominates our thinking instead of the living God. There can be so many other distractions in our lives that we are not wholeheartedly following him.

The challenge is to be like Caleb and to be wholeheartedly focused on God. The living God is to be enthroned in the centre of our vision.

The third point I want to draw out from these chapters is *the faithfulness of God*. There are many instances that show God's faithfulness to his people, in that his promises were being perpetually fulfilled.

Have you noticed how easy it is to trust God after you have gone through something? When you come out the other end and look back, it is so easy to see the way that God kept you. But it is a different matter when we are actually going through it. When the people of God were entering the Promised Land and faced all these enemies, it was impossible for some of them to believe that God would keep his promise. Yet when they looked back on all that God had done, they saw he had been faithful in this.

In Joshua 20 we come to the fourth significant point: *God instructed them to provide cities of refuge*. We read how the Lord said to Joshua, 'Tell the Israelites to designate cities of refuge as I instructed you through Moses, so that anyone who kills a person accidentally and unintentionally may flee there and find protection from the avenger of blood.' This was the most sophisticated clemency system in the ancient world. There were no other systems as advanced. Elsewhere if you did something wrong, even if it was an accident, you were punished for it. But God said there must be cities established where you could find refuge.

To those who feel pursued by evil, engulfed by problems and pain, overwhelmed by the experiences of life, God points gently to the city of refuge that we find in his presence. He loves us and longs for all in these difficult circumstances to be surrounded by the great walls of his compassion and concern, providing a place where we will be protected from Satan, from the world, and even from ourselves.

In 1762 a hospital worker named Samuel Jarvis published a very famous hymn. He had seen disease, pain and death in all their horror, yet he was able to write, with complete conviction:

How firm a foundation, ye saints of the Lord,
Is laid for your faith in his excellent word.
What more can he say than to you he hath said;
You, who unto Jesus for *refuge* have fled.

Right there, in all the pain of that unsophisticated, under-resourced hospital in the eighteenth century, he saw Jesus as his refuge.

Chapters 13-21 of the Book of Joshua have much to say to us. But the four points worthy of note and attention are these which we have looked at: people may change, but God's work goes on; the faithful, wholehearted follower will be rewarded by God; God is faithful and keeps his promises; there is a place of refuge for all who come to God.

16

The five-point law
Joshua 22:1-5

In the first chapter of Joshua the Reubenites, the Gadites and the half-tribe of Manasseh were given the land to the west of Jordan as their inheritance. But, in loving commitment to the rest of the children of Israel, they went over the Jordan and fought in the battles of Jericho, Ai and others, helping their fellow Israelites to subdue the land. Now, however, the land was largely conquered, so Joshua told them:

> 'You have done what Moses the servant of the LORD commanded, and you have obeyed me in everything I commanded .... Now that the LORD your God has given your brothers rest as he promised, return to your homes ... But be very careful to keep the commandment and the law that Moses the servant of the LORD gave you' (22:2-5).

Moses is called 'the servant of the Lord' a number of times (verses 2, 4). Moses was a great leader, yet he is not described as 'Moses who did everything wonderfully and was fantastic'. He is described as 'Moses, the servant of the living God'. These references contrast the servanthood nature of Moses and the almightiness of the living God. It is interesting that Moses' greatness was perceived in terms of his servanthood.

Many Christians, sadly, see greatness in the way the world sees it: in terms of status, of great claims, of people noticing and paying attention to us. Yet Jesus himself understood his role in terms of servanthood: he was the Servant-King. He came to serve, not to be served. In the upper room he took off his robe and, like a slave, washed the disciples' feet (John 13).

Moses was only great because he did the Master's bidding. All who aspire to leadership must see it in terms of serving: to use the small or large gifts that God has given them to release others into what they can do for God.

Five phrases in this passage summarize the meaning of the law that Moses, the servant of the Lord, had given them:

> 'To love the LORD your God, to walk in all his ways, to obey his commands, to hold fast to him and to serve him with all your heart and all your soul' (22:5).

These five commands form the basis for a secure walk with God, and are as valid at the end of the twentieth century as they were all those years ago. The first is an introductory command: 'Love the LORD your God'; the next three relate to the past, present and future: 'Walk in all his ways', 'Obey his commands', 'Hold fast to him'; and the fifth is a concluding summary command: 'Serve him with all your heart and all your soul'.

Holding to these five principles will help believers remain on track. There are many situations where we can see their value. Maybe we have to go away on work for weeks or months at a time, or have to miss church for a particular reason. We find ourselves separated from the people of God. Or perhaps we have had to miss out on the home group meeting for two or three times in succession because of pressure of work or illness or family circumstances. And all of a sudden,

we are vulnerable and Satan can get in. We need to remind
ourselves of these five principles.

Love the LORD your God

It is interesting that obedience was seen in terms of *love*. Do
you love God? By this I do not mean, Are you a Christian?
But do you love God? On one occasion, after his resurrection,
Jesus asked Peter three times, 'Peter, do you love me?'

I can imagine the tribes of Reuben, Gad and Manasseh
being puzzled by this first command. After all, they had
followed and served God. However, Joshua was highlighting
the very important difference between an understanding of
faith which is purely cerebral (I will do what God tells me to
do because I think it is right), and faith which is a relationship
with God involving the passionate response of our hearts to
him.

Christianity is often portrayed as a transaction, as a
business deal. We come with all our sin and guilt and shame;
we give God our sin and he gives us his grace and forgiveness.
This is a glorious transaction, on the basis of a contract signed
at a place called Calvary. But faith is not only an exchange of
our sins for his forgiveness and eternal life. It is also a
relationship with God who loves us and we, in turn, are called
to love him.

Sometimes, although we have committed ourselves to
Christ, having done all the things it takes to become a Christian,
our hearts are still cold because we do not have a strong love
for him. Certainly in most relationships, parents to children,
children to parents, husbands to wives and so on, it is possible
to go through the motions of fulfilling our responsibilities
without any love being involved. In fact sadly, some

relationships do continue cold and barren for many years; the outward form of relationship is there, but the heartbeat is gone. Love is not a sentimental thing, rather it is a commitment of the will from which feelings will flow.

When our faith moves from being a head-knowledge and an obedience, which is absolutely right, to something which grips our being, then we will have a great deal more security. Love of God is deeper than simply a head-knowledge of him.

Walk in all his ways

This command deals with our understanding of how God operates in the past. How do we know what his ways are, apart from looking to the past, to the events recorded in the Bible, to see what he has done? Remember the way God acts, because he is consistent. There are many things God does again and again. He does not change his mind about the way he operates.

Many Christians go from spiritual commitment and faith and trust into backsliding and then back to their commitment to God. Their whole lives are spent in this futile pattern simply because they do not learn the lessons of the past. When we come out of a bad time, we say: 'I must never be so uncaring about my relationship with God again', or 'I must take care not to let my church attendance slip again', or 'I must never be so slap-dash about reading the Bible and praying again', or 'I must never be casual with sin and forget to confess it.' But perhaps only a few months later we find ourselves doing exactly the same thing again!

Remember how God operates, and walk in his ways. Learn from the past. If we forget God's dealings with us, we repeat the errors of the past.

Obey his commands

What about the present? We are told to do what he tells us to do. The key to spiritual life and growth is not complicated. There are no special techniques, despite what we might read. It is a false spirituality to imagine there is a quick fix that will turn us into super-Christians overnight. The simple day-by-day key in Scripture is to *obey* the commands of the Lord. That is the thing we find the hardest because we are stubborn, self-centred and very strong-willed.

The Bible calls us to obedience and, in seeking obedience, we will also receive power. When we seek to be obedient to God, power results; men and women are saved and healed and changed. If you really want to grow in God and move on in your faith, the key is not to seek position but to do what God tells you to do.

Sometimes we try too hard for spiritual power and spiritual life. Often we get involved in the technicalities of spiritual power; perhaps if I pray in a particular way, or seek a particular gift, or get prayed for by a particular person, or read a particular book, or do a particular thing, then I shall have power. Actually it is much easier simply to seek God and be obedient. It is not only much easier, it is the only route to genuine spiritual power.

Hold fast to him

For the future, we are to hold fast to him. God wants to go with us into his future. To hold fast to God demands an act of the will. There will be times when you will feel a million miles from God, when it seems that faith has deserted you. In your head you still believe everything you used to believe, but you feel nothing as far as faith is concerned. In these difficult times we are called by Scripture and by personal testimony, to hold on fast when we cannot see, because we will come out of those dark times into the light of his loving presence.

Wholehearted service

The fifth command is given in the summary phrase: 'And to serve him with all your heart and with all your soul.' It is Joshua's plea to these three groups to be wholehearted in their service for God: Serve him with your whole being, as you go on into the future. If we are fulfilling the first four commands we cannot help but fulfil the fifth! Serving God involves putting these things into practice – daily, determinedly and as a permanent, lifelong feature of our lives.

17

A warning against rash judgments
Joshua 22:6-34

The incident recorded in these verses is a very human story. The Reubenites, the Gadites and the half-tribe of Manasseh decided to build an altar near the Jordan on the Israelite side. Misunderstanding their motives, the whole assembly of Israel was appalled and gathered at Shiloh to go to war against them. All the tribes had been united in fighting the Canaanites, but now civil war threatened!

Before we look at the terrible misunderstanding, there are two positive things to note from the actions of the nine and a half tribes.

Firstly, they thought that the two and a half tribes were going to build another centre of worship to Yahweh, the one true God. And they saw in the establishment of this other altar by the Jordan, a rival place of worship. They knew it was blasphemous to choose to have another centre to worship God, therefore they were angry for the honour of the eternal God. Rising within them was not self-righteousness, but a holy desire to see God's honour vindicated. We ought to be impressed by their concern for the honour of the living God.

I wish that when we Christians today make mistakes it would be out of an over-enthusiastic desire to protect the honour and integrity of God and his Word. However, that rarely happens. We seem to allow his name to be maltreated and abused, and the tragedy is that our casualness in regard to the name of Jesus and to his honour is picked up by those who do not share our Christian faith. Sometimes the church has to rise up in godly anger to protect the honour of the name of Jesus. Christians must take notice of this passion in the Old Testament for the honour of God.

Secondly, the nine and a half tribes made what was actually quite a kind and generous offer under the circumstances: 'If the land you possess is defiled, come over to the LORD's land on this side of Jordan where the LORD's tabernacle stands and share the land with us' (verse 19). There was not much room left on the west of the Jordan but the nine and a half tribes would rather be crushed and uncomfortable than have the two and a half tribes dishonour the name of the Lord. They are to be commended for this practical piece of help and advice. They do not simply condemn sin, but they also provide an alternative to it.

The church of Jesus in this century has been quick to point the finger and condemn sin. It has done very little to aid those suffering from sin, or facing the consequences of it. Similarly, some individuals are very good at seeing what is wrong in the church, their house group, or community, but they are not so good at providing help and encouragement to put it right.

The church of Jesus must speak out. Christianity has not done its job when it simply points to sin; it has only done its job when it points to the Saviour. That is why evangelism is so crucial. Included in evangelism, however, is the whole social action agenda of care for those who hurt desperately because they are part of a bleeding and broken sinful world. The church must be in the forefront of offering practical help.

The accusation

Unfortunately, however, the nine and a half tribes were just plain wrong; they completely misunderstood the motives of the other two and a half tribes.

In the Lake District, there is a hill called Point Rash Judgment, so named by William Wordsworth. The story goes that on one occasion, he and his sister were standing at the top of this particular hill. It was harvest time and looking down on a lake he saw a figure in a boat, fishing. He and his sister were angered by this, as the community needed every able-bodied man to be involved in the harvest. They came all the way down to challenge the fisherman. As they came nearer to the lake, they saw an old, bent man, who had caught a few fish. When he came ashore he explained that although he simply could not stand to work, in order to contribute to the community he had spent the whole day, since before light, trying to add a small number of fish to the community's resources. Wordsworth felt so convicted for making a wrong judgment on just a superficial sighting, that he named the place, Point Rash Judgment.

Christians are very quick sometimes to make a judgment on a leader, an elder, a staff member, a house group leader, an organization leader, or someone else in the church, on the basis of what they think they know and what they think they see. They cannot put any other evidence against it, so without consultation with them, or discussion, they then tell their view to everybody else. And time and time again they are completely wrong. But unfortunately the error is never found out, and so some go on for years, harbouring grudges and negative thoughts about other people that are utterly unfounded.

Satan loves us to have this excess baggage of hurts and

pains, of bitterness and grudges, because it breeds disunity,
it breeds contempt of other believers, it breeds in our own
souls the cancer of criticism and negativism.

The response

The two and a half tribes responded with words that are half
a prayer and half an explanation.

> Then Reuben, Gad and the half-tribe of Manasseh replied to
> the heads of the clans of Israel: 'The Mighty One, God, the
> LORD! The Mighty One, God, the LORD! He knows! And let
> Israel know! If this has been in rebellion or disobedience to the
> LORD, do not spare us this day. If we have built our own altar
> to turn away from the LORD and to offer burnt offerings and
> grain offerings, or to sacrifice fellowship offerings on it, may
> the LORD himself call us to account.
>
> 'No! We did it for fear that some day your descendants
> might say to ours, "What do you have to do with the LORD, the
> God of Israel? The LORD has made the Jordan a boundary
> between us and you – you Reubenites and Gadites! You have
> no share in the LORD." So your descendants might cause ours
> to stop fearing the LORD.
>
> 'That is why we said, "Let us get ready and build an altar –
> but not for burnt offerings or sacrifices." On the contrary, it is
> to be a witness between us and you and the generations that
> follow, that we will worship the LORD at his sanctuary with our
> burnt offerings, sacrifices and fellowship offerings. Then in the
> future your descendants will not be able to say to ours, "You
> have no share in the LORD."
>
> 'And we said, "If they ever say this to us, or to our
> descendants, we will answer: Look at the replica of the LORD's
> altar, which our fathers built, not for burnt offerings and
> sacrifices, but as a witness between us and you."
>
> 'Far be it from us to rebel against the LORD and turn away

from him today by building an altar for burnt offerings, grain
offerings and sacrifices, other than the altar of the LORD our
God that stands before his tabernacle' (Joshua 22:21-29).

Here we have ancient Israel providing a wonderful example
for modern men and women of real people grappling with
interpersonal and inter-group relationships.

To be misunderstood you have to be doing something.
People in positions of responsibility and authority are always
in danger of being misunderstood. How do they respond when
they are misunderstood? For many the tendency is to sink
into self-pity, and to wallow in the 'poor me' syndrome. They
may even display the Elijah complex, giving the impression
that there is nobody else serving God in the world. The two
and a half tribes could easily have responded by going into a
kind of corporate sulk. When I am sulking I try to pretend that
I am being profound! We try to disguise the way we are feeling
because we know only children sulk; mature Christians do
not have moods!

There are three principles that we can draw from the tribes'
response that show us how to handle being misunderstood.

1. *What God thinks matters more than what people think*.
Notice the tribes cry: 'The Mighty One, God the LORD, he
knows.' Their immediate response is not to turn to a human
arbitrator, or to call someone to their defence. No, they appeal
to God's view of the situation.

I find that when I am misunderstood, and I have had my
fair share of that as has anyone in leadership, the first step is
to take the matter back to God. I say: 'God, your view of my
life is more important than any human judgment upon it.

Others may criticize or ridicule or misunderstand something I am supposed to have said or done. Yet you know my motives; you know my aspirations. Lord, you know I want to be right in your sight.'

As Christians, our first response to being misunderstood must not be the one that comes naturally to us – to strike out or to sulk; our response must be to turn the whole thing back to God. And it is tremendously releasing when we understand that.

These two and a half tribes were at pains to know that God understood their motives for building the altar. Even if they had been misunderstood by humans, God at least, in the judgment of history, would vindicate them because their motives were right in his sight. It is important for those in leadership in the church not to be seeking the approval of men and women but to seek the approval of God. There is a danger for Christian leaders to be appeasers and compromisers, seeking always to please other Christians rather than seeking to please God.

It is also important that we take the misunderstanding to God before we share it with a fellow Christian. Sometimes if people are nice to us when we have been misunderstood, we wallow in self-pity even longer. If we have been hurt by someone and share our hurt with somebody else, and they say: 'How could you fail to be anything but hurt by this?', we sink deeper into self-pity.

Leaders do not need individuals that will stroke their egos and pretend to agree all the time. Sometimes what we need most is a rugged maturity. God wants leaders who are grown up! There will be pain, there will be problems, if we are going to mature in the things of God. There will be suffering, there will be pressure, there will be misunderstanding. There is no escaping that. If we try to live our whole lives without ever risking being misunderstood, we will be so careful we will never say anything prophetic or strong or clear.

2. *Admit you might be wrong.*

The second principle to note from the response of the tribes is that they admit the possibility of error. If what they had done had been in rebellion or disobedience, then they deserved to be judged. Some of us, when we are criticized, are so arrogant that we do not even admit to the possibility that we might have got it even a little bit wrong.

Sometimes I am criticized when I think I am 99% right, but the 1% for which I am guilty still needs to be confessed to God. There is no point in saying, 'I am 99% right.' I still need to be saying sorry to God for anything in me which is not what he wants it to be. We do need to be ready to say sorry to God and to others a great deal more quickly than we often are. Stubborn pride often stops us confessing to God and others; it is the blockage through which the Spirit longs to come and bring us healing.

3. *Speak with humility.*

The third feature of the tribes' response is their humble tone. They revealed a sense of gentleness, the irenic spirit that tries to make peace between people.

In the national Christian scene in our country, people fall into quite distinct groups. It is interesting for they are not theological groupings, they are personality types. There are those who long for reconciliation and friendship and bridge-building, and they are always looking for areas of commonality. They are looking for what they can affirm in you. And there are others who are prickly, who are always looking for the difference between them and you. They are always trying to split hairs so that they can find something to disagree with you about.

In these situations, the things that really matter, such as loving Jesus, having our sins forgiven and witnessing to others of his love, can get pushed out of sight.

God's desire for his church is for us to be involved in a humble, bridge-building ministry, looking for what we can affirm in each other, rather than what we can deny and criticize.

Now we need strength to implement these three principles. None of us has the strength to be godly. Only the Holy Spirit can give us that, which is why we need to pray for the release of the Spirit into our lives to help us.

The witness

When Phinehas the priest and all the leaders heard what the Reubenites, the Gadites and the half-tribe of Manasseh had to say they were pleased and very relieved: 'Today we know that the LORD is with us, because you have not acted unfaithfully towards the LORD in this matter. Now you have rescued the Israelites from the LORD's hand... And they talked no more about going to war...' (22:31, 32).

So instead of the altar symbolizing division, it came to stand for the unity of God's people. 'The people of Reuben and Gad said: "This altar is a witness to all of us that the LORD is God." And so they named it "Witness"' (22:34, GNB).

At the end of his long life, Joshua says that God is faithful. Joshua details what God had done for his people. It will be wonderful to be able to look back on our life and see how faithful God had been over the years. The things we worried might happen, ninety per cent of them did not. And some of the things we did not worry about, did happen. Just as he was with Joshua for all of his life, so he promises to be with us from the moment of conversion to when we pass over into his presence for ever. He is the faithful God.

Tom Chisholm was a Kentucky farmer who tilled the land in very difficult circumstances. A Methodist by upbringing he struggled to know what God was wanting to do with him. He just could not find the way forward as a farmer, so eventually he became a journalist, writing for a paper that looked at the whole farming community. He was still crying out to God that he would guide him and show him what he was supposed to do. There were times when God seemed a million miles away and there were times when God seemed very close; but Tom hung on to the fact that God had something for him. Ultimately he stopped being a journalist and went into the Methodist ministry and began to preach the gospel. At that point, he discovered that over the years of farming on the small Kentucky farm and working in journalism, God had been preparing him for this point when he would be involved in this kind of ministry. He came into a new fulfilment and a new release spiritually as the faithful God he had hung on to in the bad times ultimately showed him what he was supposed to be about. And out of that hanging on to God, Tom Chisholm wrote a hymn:

Great is thy faithfulness, O God my Father,
There is no shadow of turning with thee.

18

Joshua's farewell advice
Joshua 23:1-16

In Joshua 23, we see a man coming to the end of his life, and doing it gracefully. Many people when old become bitter, twisted and cantankerous. On the other hand, many Christians age with graciousness and maturity; all their harshness becomes softened and they become gentle, as God reveals the fruit of suffering over the years. I have met a number of men and women in their 70s and 80s in whom God has so powerfully been at work that there is a gloriousness about their maturity which I envy and covet for myself.

Even at the end of his life Joshua showed he was a positive affirmer to the people. Many leaders cannot let go gracefully. They hang on to the bitter end, leaving strife and negativity behind. A future generation cannot come through to take up the reins because the aged leaders do not know when to let go. May God help today's leaders to know when the time has come to hand on to others, to let them pick up the baton and carry on. Joshua knew when to let go, and he gave a gracious, positive, powerful, affirmatory speech in which he draws these future leaders into his own fulfilment.

Why was Joshua so gracious? Why was he so positive? Because he had continued to walk with God. He had been fulfilled in his relationship with God because he had given his life to the right thing.

We only have one life and it will soon be over. I am not being morbid, simply facing the facts. It is important, from time to time, to assess what are we doing with our lives. Are we devoting our time and energy to the things which are important?

Joshua had given his life to the conquest of the land after forty years wandering in the wilderness preparing for that task. Because he was God's servant, he found fulfilment, not in doing things that somebody else thought he ought to do, but in doing what God wanted him to do. The tragedy for many Christians is that they end up disenchanted and disgruntled because they have not actually focused on doing what God wanted throughout their lives. They may have been successful financially, or in terms of influence or status. But because they did not focus on what God wanted, they are disgruntled and unfulfilled. Many spend their whole lives climbing up the ladder, trying to get to the top only to find when they get to the end of their lives that the ladder is leaning against the wrong wall.

Why was Joshua able to be so positive to these other leaders who were going to take over? Do you know the temptation that comes when other leaders are taking over? The temptation is to be patronizing and paternalistic: 'Now boys, when you have been in this game as long as I have, you'll understand that there are a few things that you need to know about how to cope with different issues. Here are twenty lessons that I've learned and if you do it like I did it, you'll be all right.'

Actually the people could have told Joshua when he was eighty that it was time to find a new leader. But they would have been quite wrong, because God had more for Joshua to do after he was eighty than he had before it. So it is not a question of physical age, rather it is about knowing the right time to let go and to hand over to others. I know some people who are twenty going on seventy-five. Moving out of leadership has nothing to do with physical age, it is to do with attitudes, and with flexibility and openness to God.

There are three things mentioned by Joshua which are valid life-principles today, and which will stand potential leaders in good stead as they progress to maturity. These principles also have a practical application for churches too, because corporately they are important.

As we face the future, who knows what will happen. We are not far away from the end of the century, and who knows what the next one will bring. In many ways, we are still moral adolescents, for our moral and spiritual development has not been able to keep pace with the incredible scientific and technological advances which we see all around us. So we are facing incredible changes. However, the advice Joshua gave will give us a strong foundation from which to face the future.

1. *Leaders to resolve to serve God*

Joshua's first words of instruction to the new leaders were: 'Be very strong' (verse 6). The foundation for consistent Christian life and witness for leaders of a church is a determination to depend on the power of God. It has to do with resolution, to stick to what is right. There are echoes here of Joshua chapter 1 where Joshua was told to be strong and very courageous, in other words, to be resolute.

The point of resolution in Scripture is not the strength of the emotion, but its object. 'Resolute' is an adjective whose meaning can change depending on whom it is applied to: it can mean strong-willed, it can mean pig-headed.

Christians, both leaders and lay people, need to avoid being stubbornly and resolutely committed to the wrong things. Some get a bee in their bonnets about a particular issue and become blinkered to everything else. Unfortunately people like this are not always balanced in their commitment and understanding. This, however, is not the kind of strength or resolution that Joshua is referring to.

These are often individuals who by virtue of their personality are more likely to be resolute and determined. Often they do not wish to be confused with the facts, they are not remotely interested in what the truth is. These individuals are impossible, not just for other people, but for God too: they are committed to the wrong thing.

The positive side to all this is that God is looking for those people who go on resolutely, following him in the good times and in the bad, who are not going to drift away from the key anchor points of strong Christian commitment.

Many believers, including those in leadership, take their walk with God for granted, and do not understand the satanic powers ranged against them. Christians are involved in spiritual warfare. We need to look to ourselves. The Socratean advice – 'Know thyself' – is very important for Christians. We can easily become casual in our spiritual lives, believing everything is fine, without recognizing the forces ranged against us and the need for resolution, for courage, for commitment in the good times and in the bad.

Sadly even leaders can be caused to lose their footing by almost anything. Many are balanced precariously on the tightrope of Christian faith, so when the slightest challenge faces them, they lose their balance, spiritually, instead of holding on to the resources that God gives. British Christianity is breeding a whole generation of neuroticized Christians, knocked off balance by anything and everything. So Joshua's words to 'Be very strong' were timely then and are still timely now.

2. *A set of behaviour patterns for leaders*

Joshua then tells these leaders who will take over from him: 'Be careful to obey all that is written in the Book of the Law of Moses, without turning aside to the right and the left.' The Book of the Law of Moses would include the Ten Commandments and various other rituals about religious celebration and ceremonial laws. It also included laws about ethics, moral values and behaviour, relationships at work, marital relationships and so on. It was a series of rules that regulated ordinary life.

Joshua says to them that their moral standards as leaders will determine ultimately the way people behave, and the way the people will behave, he says later on, will determine whether God blesses them or not. Thus leaders should behave in godly and righteous ways. When God examines leadership roles, he not only looks for resolute determination, but also for a moral lifestyle that reflects his call in their lives.

The dichotomy between private morality and public position is not available to the Christian leader. There is a moral imperative in their lives which means that it is no use for any leader to say that what he does in private is his own affair, particularly if it is 'an affair'. If he is morally unbiblical in his private life, that affects what he says on public platforms.

One of the fundamental dangers for those who preach regularly is that they are likely to preach a great deal better than they live. They can be intoxicated with the power of words. Because of that they can very easily substitute talking about holiness for being holy. They can lead a Bible study on being filled with the Spirit and not be filled with the Spirit themselves. Helmut Thielicke, a German theologian, drew a strong word picture of preachers who build a house with the roof of prayer, the walls of Bible reading and the foundations of evangelism, and then do not live in the house which they have constructed for others, but simply view it from the outside. That, of course, is hypocrisy.

Both the member in the pew and the person in the pulpit have an equal responsibility before God for moral right-eousness. But the implications in the lives of others are more profound when leaders fall. Pray for your leaders that they will be morally righteous and have godly integrity.

3. *Leaders called to religious integrity*

Joshua's third message of advice was to remind these leaders not to associate with those nations that remained in Canaan, nor to invoke the names of their gods, or swear by them, or serve them or bow down to them. In other words, the leaders were not to be compromised theologically. Not only were they to avoid moral compromise, they were also to avoid compromise in the way they were to carry out the worship of God. This is important because theological error often leads to moral failure. The two are very closely linked.

Leaders are to be committed to the worship of the one true God whatever distractions or heresies tempt them. Today, we are in a world where there are a whole range of religious options on offer, and if leaders are not careful they can become unduly influenced by these non-Christian sources and so develop unbiblical views of a range of things.

Notice in verse 12 that there is a 'carrot and stick' approach as Joshua continues. He is either encouraging them – and that is the framework of this speech – or he is threatening them. This method seems to be quite an effective leadership policy; it is certainly used by most parents with a fair degree of success when it comes to disciplining their children.

The consequence of wrong behaviour

In verses 12-13 there are strong words. Joshua uses the word 'snare' which in the Hebrew describes a very cruel trap for an animal, involving a sharpened stick which, when the animal trod on the trap, would skewer the animal to the ground where it would writhe until it died or the hunter came along. It was a brutal death. So the picture of the snare used by Joshua is not of a harmless trap where an animal is only caged. Joshua was warning the Israelites that if they departed from God, the Canaanite inhabitants still left in the land would become like a skewer in them. But there is more: 'If you violate the covenant of the LORD' – if they broke their promise – 'then God will not protect you in the way that he has in the past' (verse 16).

Joshua is simply saying that actions have consequences. If we break the law of gravity by leaping off a cliff top, the natural consequence is a great fall followed by a big bump at the bottom. There is no good leaping off the top and then being disappointed that the law of gravity comes into effect. If we disobey God we should not be surprised that our action has a consequence, and the consequence is that God will not help us.

Christians today live in a world where people do not want

their actions to have consequences. There is a sad trend in all aspects of our society where people always blame somebody else for what has happened in their lives. Christians must resist this trend, because whenever we blame someone else and not ourselves, we cannot deal with the problem. It is not until we realize that we are sinners in the sight of God that we can confess our sin and have it dealt with. And it is a wonderfully liberating experience.

As Christians, too, our actions have consequences. If, for months or years at a time, we neglect to read the Bible and to pray, the consequence is that our spiritual lives are starved. But when we pray and read the Scriptures and try to walk with God, even when we feel weak, God blesses and strengthens us because we have done the right things. Our actions produce the consequences of spiritual strength even when we feel very weak. This is why when a Christian feels broken, what actually happens is that he or she is much stronger than he or she would have thought. Just being obedient to God over a number of years produces spiritual maturity.

A word of encouragement

The main thrust of Joshua's words to the new leaders is not negative at all. Joshua reminds them in verse 9: 'The LORD has driven out before you great and powerful nations. To this day no-one has been able to withstand you. One of you routs a thousand.' He is not saying that every Israelite could kill a thousand people. Rather he is saying that God is with them and so their numerical weakness did not matter. The odds against them were high in human terms, but what made the difference was that God was with them because he loved them.

In verse 14 Joshua says: 'You know with all your heart and soul that not one of all the good promises the LORD your God gave you has failed. Every promise has been fulfilled. Not one has failed.' These leaders had to face up to Joshua's soon departure from them by death. Maybe they felt vulnerable and insecure, just as we do at various transitional points in our lives when we are moving from security to insecurity.

Young people come to the point of leaving home for the first time, and that can be a period of great insecurity. Up till then they have looked to their parents for leadership. I had not realized how hard my mother worked on my behalf until I actually left home.

Perhaps you are facing the threat of unemployment and you fear for your future. Or perhaps you are suffering the agonies of bereavement, where, although the death may be some way in the past now, the sense of insecurity and loss is just catching up with you, and you are feeling alone.

It may be that older people are on the verge of being housebound and feel increasingly isolated and marginalised from what is happening in the community.

Perhaps there are others who feel in transition in terms of health. Something is wrong with their body, tests have been carried out and they are anxiously awaiting the results.

People in all these types of situation have gone from the security of what was, to the insecurity of the unknown. The future holds a question mark. But that is exactly the problem that is being addressed by Joshua. God has a word of encouragement for them: Jesus is the same yesterday, today and for ever. God is reliable. We can have a deep-seated confidence that our destiny is in the hands of God. His promises are true and he will not fail us.

In verse 11 Joshua highlights the main requirement God has for his people: 'Be very careful to love the Lord your God.' The issue for leaders, as well as for others, is not simply a commitment to an objective series of truths such as we find in Scripture. It is that, but it is deeper, more profound, in that we are called to love God. Sadly there are true Christian leaders who have substituted orthodoxy for life. They are right in doctrine, but there is no passion or love. They need the reality of a heart that beats in love for God.

19

Renewing the covenant
Joshua 24:1-28

Joshua 24 relates how the covenant was renewed at Shechem, involving Joshua on the one hand and the people of God on the other. Shechem is significant, for it was there that Abraham had originally been promised the land. Shechem was in the valley between Mount Ebal on one side and Mount Gerizim on the other. It was there that Joshua himself had reviewed the covenant the Israelites had made with God (Joshua 8:30-35). The location was a huge natural amphitheatre in which Joshua's voice would have carried powerfully to the people.

As Christians we need to remind ourselves of the numerous covenant commitments we have made. The most important of these is that we are covenantly committed to God. We gave him our sin and he gave us forgiveness. The price was death on the cross. Jesus paid the price for the contract in blood and so believers are in covenantal relationship with God.

We are used to legal phrases of contract; a marriage contract, for example. Archaeologists have discovered that these are nothing new: the Hittites had a form of treaty called a suzerain treaty, in which a more powerful king would make a treaty with a weaker king, the stronger providing protection for the weaker. Joshua 24 reads like one of those ancient legal contracts, except that one of the signatories is God. Joshua was reminding the Israelites that they were in a covenant relationship with God.

That means that Christians worship God on the basis of contractual, covenant commitment. God, on the other hand, is committed contractually to continue loving his people even if they sin. Now that is something worth knowing, and we are called on that basis to be covenantly committed to him.

Another commitment that flows from the covenant is the commitment believers have made to church membership. Things will occur in church life that will annoy us. But the question is not our mood or our pride, it is a question of our covenant commitment.

Joshua recorded how good God had been throughout their past history (verses 1-13). Why does he repeat what they already knew about how good and faithful God had been over the years? I am convinced that he did so as an antidote to human psychology. Most of us when we are facing the future exaggerate the problems, and when we are facing the past we exaggerate the blessings. We speak of the good old days. So Joshua was keen to remind the people about all that God had done in order to affect the way they thought of the future.

Joshua knew they had problems ahead of them. They were in a land which was not yet entirely subdued. But they were to remember what God had done. Joshua reminded them that there were times when they had failed. He reminded them that what they now possessed was given to them by God. God was with them, enabling them to conquer their enemies. They were not to forget to thank him.

This is a reminder to us too to be thankful for what God has done in us, and not take pride in what happens when we have prayed about it beforehand. Instead of complaining and moaning (common characteristics of Christians), we are called to fresh gratitude for what we have in Christ. Gratitude needs to flow in abundance because the covenantal commitment works best in a heart of thanksgiving.

On the basis of gratitude to God, Joshua called the people to a renewed commitment: 'Now fear the LORD and serve him with faithfulness' (verse 14). True love is expressed in faithfulness. Genuine love is not fickle. God's love for us is not transient or passing. It is not like a juvenile infatuation, up one minute, down the next.

God is utterly faithful but sadly, often the people of God are fickle and transient in their love for him. There are days when God is in, and we have no problems loving him; but there are other days when God is decidedly out. Another day it will be different again. We are so immature in our love for God that we have the characteristics of a teenage romance as opposed to the faithfulness of mature love.

God calls us to respond to his love faithfully in both the good and the bad times. If this is a contract, it is not simply to be expressed when we feel happy with God or are in the right 'mood' to love him. It is a faithfulness which is to be expressed at every point; whether it is convenient or inconvenient, whether we feel like loving God or not, whether we feel well or unwell. God is worthy of our worship and service in all of these extremes.

At the end of the day, the people who made a difference in Israel's history, and the men and women who make a difference in the church today, are those whose lives are characterized by stability and faithfulness. They are not eight-day wonders; they are persistent, consistent servers of the living God, whatever their feelings and moods dictate.

From verse 14-27, we find two characteristics of believers who are about to pick up the baton of leadership. Joshua says to the people: 'Fear the LORD and serve him with all faithfulness.' I want to look at both of these in more detail before going on to look at a promise to all believers.

Fearing the Lord

I already commented on this important aspect of Christian living in chapter 6. But I want to stress it again for this attitude is an antidote to much of modern church culture. Of course there is a wrong kind of fear. I have been in a number of countries where fear is so strong, you can almost reach out and touch it: fear of authority, fear of death, fear of betrayal, fear of imprisonment, fear of torture. But Joshua was not saying they ought to be terrified of the living God. The fear he wanted is closely linked with 'awe' or 'respect' in its deepest form.

The true God is different from the gods of the nations. LORD is the translation of Yahweh, the ever-living God. He is the great God, who always was, who always will be, who has the whole of the universe in his hand, and who is to be feared. We live in a society in which authority is challenged, and not respected. Even God does not have the respect due to him in our culture, sadly, not even among the people of God. Many have become altogether too chummy with the Almighty. Some in their joy and exuberance in worship, in their informality with God as a Father to his children, have lost that sense of awe of the almightiness of the living God.

Notice the phrase, 'throw away the gods', in verse 14. How could they throw them out? Because the gods were small statuettes that they could pick up and get rid of. Many believers are, in the words of James Packer, pygmy Christians because they have a pygmy God. The Israelites needed their vision of

God to be expanded and enlarged so that they would see him as the great conqueror of Jericho, Ai and other places. Today we need our horizons lifted beyond the mundane and the ordinary to the magnificence of God.

Our society has trivialised so much and brought everything down to the lowest level. The antidote to this trivia is to be presented with a vision of a splendid, almighty God who is worthy of our worship and our praise. We must move away from the comic book mentality of living, to the splendour of the God who made the world and who delivered his people. The whole Book of Joshua is a tribute to the almighty power of God against the nations of the world. I long for the church in Britain to capture the splendour of the living God in its celebrations of praise.

Faithfulness to God

Earlier in this chapter I referred to faithfulness as an important expression of the covenant. Faithfulness is desperately needed in modern culture. People are committed to something only for a while and then they move on.

Even in the church we are transient. We initially are totally committed to issue X, then only six months later some have gone off to issue Y. In the last twenty years we have ridden a rollercoaster of issues and, in the main, dealt with none of them properly. There has been emphasis on healing, on signs and wonders, on prayer concerts, on prophecy, and much else. But all many have had is a taste of each, then they moved on to something else before they have understood what God was saying to them.

Faithfulness means that the church, especially its leaders, models a commitment to truth regardless of whether it is palatable or not, and regardless of whether it is popular or not. That is why Paul told Timothy to preach the word in season and out of season. That is why Joshua was calling the people of God to a renewed faithfulness, a loyalty to the Word of God.

Believers today, influenced by the spirit of the age, move on from one thing to another with great casualness. That is why church-hopping is more popular today than it has ever been. People come to a church and stay for a while, but when the church does something they do not particularly like they move on to somewhere else. They are very casual in their commitment to a body of God's people.

But in a world where there is pressure to defect from Christianity, God calls his people to a new level of faithfulness. We have to be faithfully committed to serving and knowing and loving the Lord.

A call to fresh allegiance to God

Joshua drew a metaphorical line in the sand, and said: 'As for me and my house, we will serve the LORD' (verse 15). He invites the Israelites to a commitment of allegiance.

> 'If serving the LORD seems undesirable to you, then choose for yourselves this day whom you will serve, whether the gods your forefathers served beyond the River, or the gods of the Amorites, in whose land you are living...'
>
> Then the people answered, 'Far be it from us to forsake the LORD to serve other gods! It was the LORD our God himself who brought us and our forefathers up out of Egypt, from the land of slavery, and performed those great signs before our eyes... We, too, will serve the LORD, because he is our God' (24:15-18).

The Roman soldiers used to take an oath of allegiance to the emperor when they enrolled in the army. It was called a *sacramentum*, a promise, an oath of commitment to their commanding officer. Sometimes baptism and the Lord's Supper are called sacraments. They are pledges of committing ourselves to serving and following and loving God. The Lord's Supper should be the regular occasion for re-pledging our allegiance to our commanding officer, the Lord Jesus.

Joshua deeply desired that the people understood the seriousness of their pledge of allegiance. He was keen that it would not be a superficial commitment. Therefore he reminded them that God would not tolerate unfaithfulness: 'You are not able to serve the LORD. He is a holy God; he is a jealous God. He will not forgive your rebellion and your sins' (24:19). Joshua did not mean God would never forgive them, but he meant: 'Look, if you promise to serve God, he will keep you to it. But he is a jealous God. He won't share your allegiance with anyone else. He won't share his glory with anyone else. He is jealous.' The issue at stake here is pluralism. The Lord will not be one God among many. He is jealous for our affection and attention, and is calling us to a single-minded devotion to him.

Verse 16 records the Israelites' answer to Joshua: 'Far be it from us to forsake the LORD to serve other gods.' And they recalled how God had delivered them and protected them. They were looking back as they said that. It is so much easier to look back than to look forward.

The children of Israel were being reminded that God was with them even though they were about to go on without Joshua. It must have been difficult for them to contemplate being without the leader who had been with them through the wilderness and led them through the years of conquest. It is quite a task to face the future without your leader. God will raise other leaders, of course, but it is a feature of the people of God, that when a minister leaves a church, when a leader leaves a Christian organization, when a house group leader takes time off, the result is a feeling of nervousness and tension. The value of such situations is that they help us see where our trust lies. Is it in the leader? Or the leader's God?

Friendship and affirmation of leadership are appropriate, but always our focus should be beyond the human and on the divine; people will fail us, even the very best people. Joshua knew that and so he constantly focused on God. He does not say on this occasion: 'Look what I did for you. Wasn't I an absolutely fantastic leader?' He says, 'Look what God did.' Any good leader will point away from himself to the God we serve, and to the Scriptures that guide. All discipleship must ultimately point people to God, and not to the discipler. If that does not happen, disappointment will take place. Far too much pastoral care actually focuses people's attention towards the human agency. We do need to be human support agencies for one another, but we must never be a substitute for the divine agent. If we are, we rob people of the opportunity to exercise faith in God to help them. We must always be pointing people back to the God who is the God of all believers as well as the God of Joshua.

So the Israelites were going to praise God for all he had accomplished and they were going to continue serving him (verse 18). But Joshua challenges them to make absolutely sure they mean business. He asked the Israelites to throw away their foreign gods and yield their hearts to their Lord. The call to repentance is always a call to *do* as well as to *believe*.

There is no point in saying sorry to God if our lifestyle

does not change in response to what he is saying. The Word of God calls us to move from simply talking about getting right with God, or even standing in his presence and making a commitment, to putting our words into practice, setting things right which actually are wrong. When our allegiance is truly focused on God and our relationship with him is right, we benefit, because then we will know that God then loves us thoroughly and fully. When we are diffuse in our commitments we do not feel the full passion of God's love for us.

Travelling light is something that we Christians do not do very well. Over the years of our Christian walk we have picked up a lot of unnecessary baggage: a hurt caused by somebody; a lie told about us or to us; a disappointment caused by not being given the responsibility we expected, and so on. All these experiences are like barnacles stuck to the bottom of a boat. They cling to us and slow us down in our Christian lives. God wants us, by his power, to scrape off the barnacles from the bottom of the boat, to get rid of all the rubbish that accumulates, so that we can move more quickly in the direction he wants us to go. Far too many of us are carrying foreign gods, and it is slowing us down in our spiritual journey. But God says: 'As you face the future, jettison the things from your past that weigh you down, so that you are ready for whatever I have for you.'

Joshua decided to give the Israelites a physical reminder of their promise to serve God. He took a large stone and set it up under the oak tree near the holy place of the Lord. Then he said to all of the people: 'This stone will be a witness against us. It has heard all the words the LORD has said to you' (24:27). The stone obviously had not heard all the words, but it was a memory-aid that would witness against them if they were untrue to God.

We have seen already that occasionally the Israelites used visible objects to help them remember what God had done for them. Sometimes we need physical reminders of what God is like. That is why a cross, for example, can be helpful to Christians because it is a physical symbol of an event that took place. There is no power in a cross; what is powerful is the death and resurrection of Jesus. A cross is a symbol of the reality that lies behind it; but it is not in itself the reality.

We need physical reminders of spiritual truths because we are human, physical people. I see members of my congregation as physical reminders of spiritual truths. I knew some of them before they were Christians, and now they are believers I see them as amazing trophies of God's grace. All believers are a physical reminder to the power of God, a physical demonstration of a spiritual reality and truth.

I would encourage you to have trigger objects in your lives, so that as you pass them, whatever they may be, you will have a constant reminder to say to yourself: 'I praise God for that.' You will identify a certain object in your mind with a need to pray, or a need to praise, or a need to give thanks to God for something particular. We can find ways of bringing the divine into the commonplace; bringing the supernatural into the ordinary and humdrum of our every day.

20

God's work goes on
Joshua 24:29-33

The Book of Joshua ends with three burials. First there is the death of Joshua:

> Then Joshua sent the people away, each to his own inheritance.
> After these things, Joshua son of Nun, the servant of the LORD, died at the age of a hundred and ten. And they buried him in the land of his inheritance at Timnath Serah in the hill country of Ephraim, north of Mount Gaash (24:29-30).

Joshua, in his leadership, had given the people of Israel value for money. He was a faithful, long-term servant of the people of God, and had given them thirty years of faithful service.

So strong was his influence that 'Israel served the LORD throughout the lifetime of Joshua and of the elders who outlived him and who had experienced everything the LORD had done for Israel' (24:31). Even though Joshua was dead, because of his influence, the people of Israel kept on being faithful for a number of years after his death.

The second burial we read of in this chapter is that of Joseph, who had died in Egypt some 400 years earlier. Before he died, he had requested that he be buried in the Promised Land: 'And Joseph's bones, which the Israelites had brought up from Egypt, were buried at Shechem in the tract of land that Jacob bought... This became the inheritance of Joseph's descendants' (24:32).

The third burial is that of Eleazar, described in verse 33: 'And Eleazar, son of Aaron, died, and was buried at Gibeon, which had been allotted to his son Phinehas in the hill country of Ephraim.'

Eleazar, Joseph and Joshua are all buried in the Promised Land, the place of their ancestry, the place they would call home.

In the Jewish faith there were three main attachments: the law, the land and, as their history unfolded, the temple. Right from the very beginning, however, probably the ultimate attachment for Jews was the land. We can see this clearly in the speech of Stephen in the Acts of the Apostles (chapter 7). In Joshua, too, the emphasis is on the land. God's people had got their land back and these three heroes of the faith find their ultimate resting place in the land that God had promised to them. Each one of them was a recipient of God's promise come true.

Whereas Joshua and Eleazar did not have to wait a long time for this to happen, Joseph, however, had to wait over 400 years. The passing of time is no contradiction to the promise of God.

Perhaps at one time you sensed you were being promised things by God, but the passing of time has eroded your confidence in his Word. Sometimes we have to wait longer than we had expected for the fulfilment of God's promise. But its reality is utterly certain. We have all been promised eternal life, those of us who know Jesus as our Saviour. Some of us will go to glory earlier than others. The reality of eternal salvation with God for ever in heaven may be deferred or delayed. Some of us will live to a very great age, but the promise, though it is slow in being fulfilled, is utterly guaranteed. We have in this passage a reminder of the certainty of the living Word of God.

It was said to me years ago: 'God buries his workmen, but carries on his work.' All of us are expendable. All of us, eventually, will die. God's work is not dependent on us as individuals, for the church of Jesus will corporately take it on into the future. Three treasured leaders were buried, but the work went on. The Israelites carried on serving the Lord. So treasure what you have now; it will not always be the same. It might be better in the future or it might be worse, but the present is all we have to give to God.